ST. MARY MAGDALENE

ABOUT THE AUTHOR

Malachi eben Ha-Elijah is a modern mystic. His spiritual journey began as a young boy, when he made the acquaintance of a Tau of the Sophian Tradition of Gnostic Christianity, Tau Elijah ben Miriam. Tau Malachi received the oral tradition of Sophian Gnosticism from Tau Elijah, and has been a student and practitioner of Gnostic Christianity for over thirty-five years. In 1983 he founded Sophia Fellowship as an expression of the tradition, and has been teaching and initiating others into Christian Gnosticism, Rosicrucian Philosophy and Christian Kabbalah since that time. He is an initiate of Ordo Sanctus Gnosis and serves as an Elder and Tau within the Sophian lineage.

Tau Malachi is also a Chevalier (a dubbed Knight) in the International Order of Chivalric Companions, a Martinist, and is an ordained and consecrated Independent Bishop. He is the founder of Ecclesia Pistis Sophia and is among the leading exponents of Christian Gnosticism and Kabbalah in our times.

Along with his exploration of the Western Mystery Tradition, he has studied extensively in several Eastern Traditions, such as Vajrayana Buddhism and Vedanta, and he also studied within a Middle Eastern Tradition of Sufism, as well as becoming involved in Native American Shamanism. Though Gnostic Christianity has always been his heart-path and spiritual home, Malachi speaks of himself as a spiritual traveler and explorer, one who seeks the Spirit of Truth everywhere it is to be found.

For many years Tau Malachi served as a hospice volunteer, a volunteer trainer, and for a period of time as a hospice chaplain. Although he worked with patients suffering from various forms of terminal illness over the years, much of his work focused on individuals suffering with HIV and AIDS.

Today he lives in the Sierra foothills, in Nevada City, California.

ST. MARY MAGDALENE

THE GNOSTIC TRADITION
OF THE HOLY BRIDE

TAU MALACHI

Llewellyn Publications
Woodbury, Minnesota

FIRST EDITION
Third Printing, 2006

Cover design by Gavin Dayton Duffy
Cover painting © by Neal Armstrong/Koralik & Associates   FR
Editing and interior design by Connie Hill

Llewellyn is a registered trademark of Llewellyn Worldwide, Ltd.

Library of Congress Cataloging-in-Publication Data
Malachi, Tau.
    St. Mary Magdalene : the Gnostic tradition of the holy bride / Tau Malachi
— 1st ed.
        p.   cm.
    Includes bibliographical references.
    ISBN-10: 0-7387-0783-X
    ISBN 13: 978-0-7387-0783-9
    1. Mary Magdalene, Saint.   2. Gnosticism.   I. Title.

BS2485.M345   2006
299'.932—dc22   2005044755

Llewellyn Publications
A Division of Llewellyn Worldwide, Ltd.
2143 Wooddale Drive, Dept. 0-7387-0783-X
Woodbury, MN 55125-2989, U.S.A.
www.llewellyn.com

Printed in the United States of America

DEDICATION

I'd like to dedicate this book to the loving memory of Mother Sarah, who, along with Tau Elijah Ben Miriam, was a teacher and guide to me in my youth, and who remains in my heart always. She was a holy woman and a Sacred Tau in the tradition.

I'd also like to dedicate it to the memory of my mother, who gave birth to me and raised me, and who facilitated my spiritual journey— who hoped all good things for me, all in the nobility of motherhood.

May this book serve as a remembrance of Sophia, the Holy Mother and Bride, in all women.

OTHER BOOKS BY TAU MALACHI

Gnostic Gospels of St. Thomas

Gnosis of the Cosmic Christ

Living Gnosis

Los Evangelios Gnósticos de Santo Tomás

CONTENTS

ACKNOWLEDGEMENTS

I must first and foremost give thanks to my beloved Teacher, Tau Elijah ben Miriam, and to his circle of spiritual companions, from whom I received the oral tradition of Sophian Gnosticism that appears in this book—all that flows out in sacred discourse and writings today come from his blessing and teachings. He was, perhaps, the best friend I will ever have in this world, and truly a holy person.

I also must thank Penelope Amadali for her loving and faithful help as a midwife in giving birth to this book in manuscript form, and to all of my spiritual companions, without whose love, encouragement and support this project could not have been completed. I am truly blessed with holy company in this life—amazing spiritual friends!

I'd also like to thank Bishops Timothy Storlie and Debra Belshee-Storlie who have helped inspire the creation of Ecclesia Pistis Sophia (Church of Faith Wisdom) as a vehicle to extend the light of the Holy Bride, Sophia, and to share the Sophian teachings recorded in this series of books. It is a privilege and honor, and a great blessing, to have entered into their acquaintance—yet more to have had the opportunity to exchange sparks of initiation with them and to call them my spiritual friends.

Last, I must also thank Llewellyn Worldwide and all of the staff at Llewellyn. They perform an immeasurable service in giving voice to peoples of alternative spirituality—without them I do not know that this voice of the Holy Bride would be heard. Their contribution to the movement of the Mother Spirit in our times cannot be adequately conveyed with words—but many people are blessed by the work they do to sponsor the communication of Light, Love, Life, and Liberty.

To everyone involved in the co-creation of this book, to include you, the reader of this book, I give my heartfelt thanks! You are deeply appreciated!

INTRODUCTION

PART ONE

The Oral Tradition

My own experience of St. Mary Magdalene began when I was a little boy. It was a beautiful spring morning and I was playing outside in the garden. A presence of light attracted my attention, and when I looked, I saw an image of the Lady in Red standing near me and smiling. Light surrounded her and she felt deeply familiar. Her presence was warm and comforting, yet, at the same time, energizing. I could hear her voice in my mind, as in a dream, and she said, "We will meet again. I am coming." Then, just as she had seemed to appear out of nowhere, she vanished, and I found myself quite accepting of what had transpired. It was as though some deeper part of me knew what had happened and what was meant, but on a conscious level, all I knew was the experience of love and delight that had come over me and that I liked what had happened. Of course, to a little boy, this did not seem strange at all, for the minds of children seem to be naturally mystical and magical.

What she said in my mind, the promise she made, she fulfilled. After that first experience I frequently encountered her in dreams and visions. Often she had variations of the same message, but on other occasions she would tell me or show me things, as though guiding me and preparing me for experiences yet to come. Until I met my Gnostic teachers of the Sophian Tradition, I did not know who she was. Like others before me, I simply called her the "Lady in Red." As anyone who has a propensity to dreams and visions understands, I swiftly learned not to speak to anyone about my experiences, but rather to keep them private. After all, people who "see" such things are "crazy," or so it is said by our unenlightened society.

It is not surprising that I stumbled across a Gnostic circle that preserved a vast oral tradition about St. Mary Magdalene. I'd have to say that behind the scenes, whether I realized it or not, she led me to it. Encountering my teachers, Tau Elijah and Mother Sarah, and the Gnostic circle that formed around them, was like coming home. I soon learned who the Lady in Red was, and I began to hear the legends about her and teachings attributed to her from my beloved teachers. Any time her tales were told, I found myself enrapt and filled with awe and wonder. I would feel her presence as I listened and heard them. The tales would inspire insights into St. Mary Magdalene and dreams and visions of her far more conscious and detailed than what had transpired before. She became to me the Living Sophia (Wisdom) and my divine muse in the spiritual path.

This is the power of the Gnostic legends of St. Mary Magdalene. They express the insights, dreams, and visions of generations of Gnostic Christians to whom Mary Magdalene is an important figure and inspiration, and they help us to connect with her and enter into the Gnostic experience of her. They are not meant to be factual in any historical sense, but rather are intended to be inspirational and experiential. They are designed to communicate spiritual and metaphysical truths about Divine reality that cannot be conveyed in any other way. Listening and hearing the legends, or reading them, is an adventure in sacred fantasy through which one might experience the same Divine illumination as those who tell the tales, and through which, in fact, one might bring forth new insights and inspiration via the play of the Creative Spirit in oneself. In other words, the Gnostic legends are akin to a guided meditation or creative visualization through which knowledge, understanding, and wisdom might be brought forth from within oneself. Thus, what they ultimately mean depends upon one's own experience of the Truth and Light they communicate and the insights and inspiration they invoke.

As one reads this book, one must bear in mind that it is a record of an oral tradition and that typically, among Sophians, it is spoken person to person rather than being written and read. In other words, the legends and sayings are a fluid and flowing body of teachings, ever in flux and ever changing with each telling of the tale. There is certainly always some degree of consistency, but there is also improvisation in the power of the moment. They are not so fixed or static as they might seem in written form. They flow out of the inspiration of the Spirit and creativity of the one who is telling the stories, and there is also inspiration and creative play in those who listen and hear the stories. Thus, when reading them, it is quite all right to read between the lines, to contract or expand the story, or even that a completely different story is inspired—it is all part of the intended process of Gnostic legends in the Sophian Tradition. It is not that we should hear them or read them as though they are some sort of creed or doctrine to be believed in blind faith. Instead, they are an invitation to an adventure in consciousness, in thought, emotion, and imagination. They point us toward a Gnostic Gospel—one we are meant to discover and receive inwardly instead of something being imposed from the outside. In the end, what we believe or disbelieve as a spiritual person must be shaped according to our own insights, our own experience of the Truth and Light—such is the Gnostic way.

To receive oral tradition in person is definitely a unique and powerful experience. I cannot say that receiving a written form is exactly the same; for when teachings and legends are spoken in person, there is a distinct experience of a living presence and power that moves with them—a tangible energy within and behind the words that forms another dimension to the transmission. Yet, ultimately, from the Gnostic perspective, it is all about facilitating a direct spiritual or mystical experience, and such Gnostic experience is dependent upon the Great and Invisible Spirit. Thus, an oral tradition placed into writing can also be a powerful vehicle of the Spirit of Truth. If one opens oneself to St. Mary Magdalene, the Holy Bride, she can and will reveal herself through a book—for what she personifies is within each and every one of us, man and woman alike. Whether a transmission is oral or written, the whole purpose is drawing out this Fiery Light from within us.

Since the time I first sat listening and hearing the Gnostic legends of St. Mary Magdalene and received my introduction to her Gospel, I have had a deep impulse to write some of them down. It has been my dream since I was a young boy. I have come to understand this desire as a wish to share my own joy as well as to preserve what I feel to be a precious Wisdom treasury of the Western Mystery Tradition. Today, more and more people are asking questions about St. Mary Magdalene and seeking to know everything they can about her. It seems that it is time for this delightful oral tradition to be made accessible. Previously, it has been preserved and cultivated in a relatively small secret society of Gnostic friends, and, by necessity, it has been hidden away and very hard to find. Her story is a great and archetypal story, although until recent times it has not been openly told—it is the story of our own soul in the process of self-realization or evolution to Christ consciousness.

PART TWO

The Sophian Tradition of Gnostic Christianity

To understand the view of Mary Magdalene held by Sophians, we must consider the Christ revelation as taught among Gnostics, for the Gnostic vision of Christ is very different than that of orthodox and fundamental forms of Christianity. According to orthodox and fundamental schools of Christian thought, the state of Christ is exclusive to Lord Yeshua (Jesus)—he is literally viewed as the "only Son of God" sent to "save" the world, and one must believe that he is the "only Son of God" in order to be "saved." In this view, he is literally believed to have been born of a virgin and born the Christ. In the Gnostic view, however, a distinction is made between Christ and the Christ-bearer. Thus, in the Gnostic view, Yeshua was born a human being, just like us, although, indeed, a very lofty soul, and he had spiritual teachers, John the Baptist being his primary teacher. During the baptism in the River Jordan, performed by John, Yeshua became Christed, which is to say that he became a realized or enlightened individual. Among Gnostics, this is the true meaning of Christ. It is a state of higher consciousness in which one becomes aware of one's innate unity with God (the Source) and, thus, experiences salvation (enlightenment and liberation). It is for this reason that Gnostics believe in salvation through gnosis, which is the product of a direct spiritual or mystical experience of the Truth that illuminates and liberates the soul. In this sense, the idea of Christ to Gnostics is similar to that of Buddha in Eastern Traditions—an enlightened being who teaches and initiates others in a path to enlightenment.

In this view the Christos, which is commonly called the "Light-presence," is not isolated to the person of Yeshua. It is within each and every one of us equally. A person must only learn to recognize and realize the Light-presence in him or herself in order to consciously embody it. Thus, in the Gnostic view, the Christos or Light-presence is not only embodied in Lord Yeshua, he teaches others how to recognize and realize it within themselves. Therefore, it was embodied in his disciples to various degrees, just as it was in him. This basic Gnostic idea is reflected in the Gnostic Gospel of St. Thomas, for example, in which we are told that the apostle Thomas is the "twin" of the Living Yeshua, which implies that he realized Christ within himself, just as Yeshua did. Likewise, it is reflected in the Gnostic Gospel entitled Pistis Sophia in which Yeshua tells his disciples that they are also "saviors." According to the Gospel of the Sophian Tradition, the first and foremost disciple to realize Christ within herself was St. Mary Magdalene. Thus, while Yeshua is the first Christed man, Mary Magdalene is the first Christed woman, and the two together reveal the divine potential in humanity and the destiny of all human beings—the attainment of Christhood.

From the Sophian perspective, the idea of the Christos being revealed exclusively in a male form, apart from the female form, is considered incomplete and goes against the very nature of our experience, for the Life-power is equally in men and women, and Christ consciousness is essentially the same whether embodied in a man or a woman. If the Christos is, indeed, a Light-presence that illuminates and liberates the soul, and is, in fact, the very nature of the soul or consciousness itself, then it is in both men and women—within everyone and everything. Therefore, according to the myth and metaphor of the Sophian Tradition, the Christos had to be revealed in both male and female form, providing both men and women with an image of Christhood to which they might aspire, as though an image of their future and Divine Self.

Thus, according to the Sophian Tradition, St. Mary Magdalene is said to be the soul mate of Lord Yeshua and becomes his closest disciple. Yet more than a disciple, she is said to be his wife and consort, co-equal and co-enlightened with him, and she is the co-preacher of the Gospel. In him, Christ the Logos (Word) is embodied and, in her,

Christ the Sophia (Wisdom) is embodied. Through their union in the mystery of *hieros gamos* (the sacred marriage), the Divine fullness of the Christos is revealed. In effect, according to the Sophian myth and metaphor, the Light of the Christos and the Gospel flows forth from their love-play.

In classical Gnostic mythology, Christ the Logos descends from the Divine reality of the spiritual world and enters into the lower realms and material world in pursuit of his female counterpart, who for one reason or another has fallen from her original state as a Divine Being. The Logos descends in order to redeem and restore Sophia to her rightful place, as well as to complete himself as Christ. Just as she is in need of him for her fulfillment, he is in need of her in order to be complete. In the Sophian Tradition, this myth plays out in the stories of Lord Yeshua and Lady Mary. Hers is the story of the fall and re-demption of Sophia. His is the story of the Logos who descends to awaken her and draw her in ascent with him, restoring her to her origi-nal state of Divine Being along with himself. Essentially, it is the story of the involution and evolution of our own soul through the process of incarnation and our eventual awakening to remember of the Truth and Light in us. Yeshua and Mary are personifications of this Truth and Light. Thus, more than historical personalities or anything external to ourselves, they must be understood to reflect something in us that we are meant to experience and to recognize and realize inwardly. It is in this context that Sophians study and contemplate the Gnostic Gospel and all associated Gnostic legends. It is to awaken and embody the Truth and Light of our inmost being and become Light-bearers in the world.

CYCLE 1

PROPHETIC REVELATIONS
OF THE BRIDE'S BIRTH

The Circle Drawer

In those days there was a circle drawer and prophet in the hills of Galilee. His name was Jeremiah and he was noted as a wonder-worker. When he cast circles, he could command the elements, he was able to commune with spirits of God and holy angels, and oftentimes he had visions of things that would come to pass.

One evening he went into a cave to pray, meditate, and contemplate the mysteries of heaven. He drew a circle and sat within it. Inwardly, he chanted the Great Name of God. Suddenly, an angel from the order of Kerubim[1] appeared at the mouth of the cave to stand guard, and a light shone from the back of the cave, as though a door to paradise had opened. In the light, Jeremiah glimpsed the image of Adam Ha-Rishon, the first human being. He beheld this person of Light become a man and woman of Light, and it was a beautiful and glorious vision of perfection. Then, behind the man and woman of Light, the supernal archangel Metatron[2] appeared, and fire and light filled the cave. A heavenly voice proclaimed, "Look! The Anointed is coming and will soon arrive, and in the body of the Anointed a new creation shall come into being!"

With these words, the true form of Metatron was revealed to Jeremiah. Hearing these words and seeing the awesome glory of the archangel, his soul leapt out of his body, as though at the time of death. A great host of angels carried his soul in ascent through the seven heavens, from one to the other, as though through chambers of a palace of lights. In his heart he cleaved to the Holy One, undistracted by any lesser glory. He was taken up in Divine rapture to the threshold of the

Supernal Abode and there was met by the spirits of Elijah and Enoch,[3] from whom it is said he received secret teachings. Then the vision of the throne of the Holy One appeared. A great luminous assembly of righteous spirits and holy angels of countless orders appeared gathered around the throne, and Jeremiah gazed into the countenance of the One-Who-Sits-Upon-the-Throne. From the heart of the Holy One upon the throne, who is the image and likeness of the glory of Yahweh Elohim,[4] a great light emanated, and it became a man and woman of Light, the image of Christ the Logos and Christ the Sophia.

A great procession formed, escorting the twins of Light in descent through the heavens and realms in between, as they made their way to earth, in which the soul of Jeremiah was caught up. A heavenly voice said to Jeremiah, "Bear witness to the Great Seth,[5] the Anointed, and the mysteries of what shall come to pass!" So it was that the soul of Jeremiah was drawn in descent with the Light-presence and witnessed the Light-presence transform to assume the appropriate appearance, resembling the beings dwelling in each dominion through which the Anointed passed. He witnessed the gestures and heard the words by which the way was opened, and knew inwardly the mysteries of the coming of the Human One into the world. He saw the man of Light enter into the world and the woman of light enter into the world after him. Then the heavenly voice said, "And so it shall come to pass; and so it is done!" All good spirits and heavenly hosts rejoiced and gave thanks and praise before the presence of Yahweh,[6] above and below.

The soul of the prophet was returned to his body, although he lay as though dead until daybreak. When he arose, he gave praise and thanks unto the Holy One of Being, and sang and danced with great joy in the presence of the Lord. The Spirit of Yahweh was upon Jeremiah and led him to the town of Magdal,[7] to the family into which the Holy Bride would be born. The mother of Our Lady believed the man of God, for she had heard of the wonders he performed, and she rejoiced in her heart. However, when the father of Our Lady heard the prophecy of a holy and anointed child, he assumed a son like King David was to be born to him, and he lusted after the wealth and power that would some day come to him. Jeremiah blessed the mother of Our Lady but did not correct the assumptions of her father, nor did he bless him. Then Jeremiah departed and went his way, knowing his soul fulfilled in bearing witness to the coming of the Messiah. Shortly thereafter Jeremiah died; his life's mission was complete and there was a greater blessing in store for him. For it is said that his soul swiftly reincarnated to be a disciple to the Anointed, and many say it was as St. Philip that he returned, one of the disciples faithful to Our Lady.

When it came to pass that his wife gave birth to a daughter and not a son, Mary's father was angry and cursed the Lord, believing the man of God a deceiver. On that very day, he decided to find a wealthy man to marry her, with the intent of sending her far away as soon as she came of age. For he thought to himself, "Even a daughter can be a boon!" He would never come to know the holy soul living in his midst, for his mind was of the world and his heart was hardened. Yet, the mother of Mary believed her daughter was a holy person, although she would not speak what was in her heart; neither when the time came would she protect her daughter. For as much as she felt her daughter was holy, she too was a woman of the world and loved things of the world. Thus, she believed a marriage to a wealthy man would be in her daughter's best interests.

The Prophet Who Was Slain

It is said that the archangel Gabriel[8] appeared to another prophet of the time to disclose mysteries of the coming of the Messiah. First, Gabriel spoke of the mysteries of the Bridegroom; then he began to speak the mysteries of the Holy Bride. When the prophet heard of a holy woman, he thought Gabriel was a demon deceiving him and he called upon the name of the Lord to banish and destroy the deceiving spirit.

When the prophet did this, Gabriel transformed into a great dragon and devoured the prophet, for it was the prophet who was the deceiver and who refused to receive the Wisdom of God. This we know from a disciple of the prophet who witnessed the event and was touched in the head thereafter, but whom later the Holy Bride would heal.

The Old Woman

An old woman of the town of Magdal saw a vision of the birth of the Holy Bride, and she rejoiced in the beauty and perfection of womanhood she beheld. From that day on, she held the Holy Bride close in her heart. She dreamed many dreams, saw many visions, and experienced visitations by holy angels. The people of the town thought the old woman had gone mad and paid her no mind. When she died, she was taken in joy by the angel of Sophia, for she had grown wise.

The Vision of Miriam's Well

A woman in Judea, who was a known prophetess, saw that Mother Mary, the Mother of Yeshua, would rediscover Miriam's well.[9] Legend says that, when the prophetess Miriam died, a great angel hid the well on the shores of the Sea of Galilee. In her vision, this holy woman saw Mary find it.

This woman knew Mother Mary and she spoke her vision to her. When Mary heard it she said, "The water of the well will be my son, and the well will be his bride." It was by the inspiration of the Holy Spirit that Mary said this. Both women rejoiced together and gave praise and thanks in the presence of the Lord, the Holy Shekinah.[10] It was on account of this that Mary recognized her daughter-in-law when they met, for from that day she dreamt of her.

Women's Intuition

When Mary Magdalene was in her mother's womb, many women recounted dreams and visions after coming around her. Often women would say to her mother, "Your child is going to be special," while others would say, "The child in your womb is a holy soul." Mary's mother felt this was true, for while Mary was in her womb, she, too, dreamed heavenly dreams and, in her dreams, experienced the visitation of angels. Yet, truly, Mary's mother did not know what to make of all of this, for she had never been inclined to the spiritual world. She was uplifted and experienced joy in her pregnancy, and she welcomed her daughter with great affection. Many say she was conflicted all of her life regarding Mary. For she could not dismiss her spiritual experiences and yet neither could she fully accept them. Thus it was a troubling in her soul all the days of her life. In truth, her soul was not of the lofty grade of Mother Mary. She had a soul of admixture; therefore, she could not fully know her daughter as Mother Mary knew her son. Indeed! The matrix through which Mary entered into the world was very different than the matrix through which Yeshua[11] entered— blessed be the Bride in her strength to overcome!

Pagan Seers

There were many in the holy land who received prophecy about the coming of the Anointed. There were also seers in foreign lands who saw visions of the Anointed and the coming of the Bride. In the new land to which Magdalene would later travel after the events of the Gospel came to pass, many holy women saw visions of the Anointed and Holy Bride. Because they were pagan and worshipped the Great Goddess, they believed she was the incarnation of the Goddess. Therefore, they prophesied of a great holy women and goddess who would come among them and who would teach them a new way of the Mother. For this reason, many years later, when St. Mary Magdalene came among them with her son, bearing the presence and power of Christ the Sophia, she was swiftly received among these people. All along, they were expecting a Light-bearer in a female form, and the Divine Mother was already known and accepted by them to some degree. These people were said to have lived in what has become known as southern France.

Visions of the Young Maiden

A young girl was experiencing dreams and visions of the Bride. She beheld a woman of light passing through realms of shadows and shades

and down into the abodes of Gehenna, from one gate to another, down
into the deepest pit of darkness. There, she beheld the Holy One
slain. She wondered at what she saw and questioned the Spirit of the
Lord, saying, "How can this be, that so bright a light shall fall into so
great a darkness?" The Mother Spirit answered her, saying, "So it is
with the human ones. All are souls of Light and are bound to a great
and terrible darkness. So it is that God's Wisdom shall enter and become as they are to enlighten and liberate them. God's Word shall
enter and take up Wisdom, that all might be set free. Unless Sophia
drew near, how should it be that any might receive God's Word? Is it
not she who sees and hears, touches, tastes, and smells, and therefore
knows by way of him and he by way of she? From the beginning, it
has been ordained, for she has led the involution of souls and he shall
lead the evolution. Yet, she shall be the fruition of all, having come
into the depths so as to know the heights." Being a sister of the Holy
Bride, the young girl understood the Holy Spirit and received comfort from her. Blessed be She-Who-Understands, for she is as our
Holy Mother.

The Annunciation of the Bride's Birth

Gabriel went to Mother Mary and announced the conception of Lord
Yeshua, he who was conceived by the love of Joseph and Mary. It is
said that the Holy One of Being also sent Gabriel to the mother of
Mary Magdalene, but she was neither able to see nor to hear the
archangel because she was blind and deaf and dumb to the spiritual
world until the holy soul of the Bride was fully in her womb. So it is
with mothers and their children, some are in harmony and some are
in opposition, and it all transpires in the Great Mother.

The Mother's Inspiration

Mother Mary visited Elizabeth, the mother of John the Baptist, and it
is said that the prophet leapt in the womb of Elizabeth when his disciple, who would become the Messiah, drew near. The Holy Mother
also sought to visit the mother of the Bride and she set out to do so,

for the Holy Spirit revealed the lights of the Gospel to her. Yet, along the way, a great angel with a sword appeared to Mary and asked her, "Mother of Righteousness, what are you doing?" She said, "Archangel, you know. I am going to meet the mother of my daughter, even as I have met with the mother of my twin son. It is ordained that I should know all of my children." The angel then said to her, "Yes, Blessed Mother, what you say is true, but until it is time, the Light and Fire cannot be mingled, and the Queen of Heaven ought not be brought into a house of darkness, sorrow, and suffering. You must turn back and let your daughter come to you, where you dwell, as it is ordained." So the Mother turned back and never went to see the mother of the Bride, for Mary lived surrendered to the Holy One of Being and knew well the wisdom of God the Mother.

Notes

1. Literally, "strong ones."

2. An archangel associated with Enoch in legend, and is said to be set above all angels.

3. Two characters from the Old Testament said to have ascended without experiencing death; also personifications of the spirit of the prophets and spirit of the initiates, respectively.

4. Typically translated "Lord God," indicates masculine and feminine aspects of God.

5. By esoteric implication, Seth means the "Light of the Cross."

6. Literally, "That Which Was, Is and Forever Shall Be."

7. Hence the name "Mary Magdalene"; Mary of Magdal.

8. Literally, "the strength of God"; archangel associated with the moon and the elements of water.

9. According to legend, this well was said to magically appear wherever the Israelites wandered in the wilderness of the desert and was connected to magical powers attributed to the prophetess Miriam.

10. A Hebrew term for the feminine presence and power of God, often called the "Consort of God" in Kabbalah.

11. Aramaic for "Jesus," the meaning of the name is "Yahweh delivers."

CYCLE 2

THE BIRTH, YOUTH, AND EARLY LIFE OF THE BRIDE

The Eve of Birth

St. Mary of Magdal was born on the eve of the Holy Shabbat,[1] coming forth from her mother's womb just as the sun
set in the gate of the west, at the time when the Tzaddikim[2]
were out welcoming the Queen of the Shabbat.[3] Though
none who were in the house where she was born had eyes to
see the luminous assembly gathered within and around the
house, there was a holy man praying in an orchard who beheld a great fire and Light come upon the earth, and he knew
the Supernal Kingdom had come. Because it was the Shabbat,
however, he could not travel, but he tended to the Shabbat as
a faithful lover of the Beloved. Needless to say, the holy man
was filled with great joy and expectation and pondered the
meaning of what he had seen.

That night, when he was with his wife alone and honoring
the Holy Shekinah with her, he had a vision of the Queen of
Heaven and her Daughter,[4] yet he saw a great divide between
them. He told his wife what he had seen. Like him, she was
bewildered. She also had seen a vision, but what she saw was
Eve and Lilith[5] and the great divide between them. She
shared her vision with him, and he was even more startled.

At midnight, as was his custom, he arose from his bed, but
on this occasion he had not slept, for as much as he was filled
with joy, he was also filled with fear and trembling. It was as
though his whole body was on fire. Thus, he sought to unify
the Great Name,[6] one letter to another, and kept vigil until
the time of morning prayer. When the sun rose on the day of
Shabbat, another vision came to him of the Anointed in
whom the Queen of Heaven was joined with the Bride and a
Great Light shining in the world. So it was that, at each time

13

of prayer, the Divine vision progressed, until at the close of the Shabbat he glimpsed the world to come.

Now, the man had his heart set on going to find the place where the Queen of the Shabbat had blessed the world. Yet once the Shabbat passed, for the life of him he could not intuit the place and the Spirit would not show him. He said to his wife, "We have glimpsed the Eternal Shabbat,"[7] and she agreed with him. She said to him, "Yes, for I saw Eve and Lilith united, and Eve restored to her place, and all souls gathered once again into the body of the Human One, all a single one."

Although neither wise men nor prophets came to the birth of the Holy Bride, there is no doubt many holy men and women perceived signs and wonders on that Shabbat. It is by grace that this story has come down to us. As it turns out, this righteous man and woman conceived a child on that Shabbat eve and she was among the women disciples of Yeshua and Mary. Some say that she was Salome,[8] the wise one.

Disturbance of the Archons

The Bridegroom was invisible to the archons,[9] but the Bride was visible. Therefore, when the Bride was born, the archons were greatly disturbed. They feared their dominion of the world would soon come to an end. Thus, on the eve of the Bride's birth, they blinded everyone who was near. The archons hardened the heart of her father and dimmed the wits of her mother so that Mary might be cast out under their dominion and her holy soul might not enter into her. Indeed! They sought to steal the power of her soul unto themselves, so that the Soul of the World and the Light of humanity would be their own. Because they were bound to the demiurgos,[10] they did not know that they served the Holy One in secret as they laid their plans and began their pursuit of Sophia. In fact, she was a distraction to them; for in pursuit of her, they did not see Logos taking root in the world and thus did nothing to stop the Divine plan until it was too late.

It has always been this way since humankind has walked in the world. The demiurgos and archons cloud the minds of human beings so that they cannot see the divinity within themselves and remain as beasts of the field, driven by hidden spiritual forces. Many speak of the dangers of Satan,[11] the great adversary, but the greater danger is the demiurgos and archons, whose influence is not so easily recognized as is true evil and darkness. So from the eve of her birth, the archons stalked the Holy Bride, seeking to defile and dominate her.

Beauty Concealing the Soul

Even as a little baby, St. Mary Magdalene was beautiful, and her intense beauty only increased as she grew from year to year toward maturity. Everyone who saw her loved her, men and women alike, because of her amazing appearance. Her complexion and form were flawless. Her olive-tone skin set off her green eyes, so that they shined like emeralds. If anyone became caught up in her gaze, they could not look away until she broke off her glance. Although gazing into her eyes and experiencing her enchanting charm, no one could see past her beauty into her heart, mind, and soul, in which there was a far greater beauty and glory. This was her plight, that no one could see her and no one knew her. Inwardly, she was alone and could not be herself. She was an object of desire. The grief and pain of this imprisonment haunted her throughout her youth and early life.

The Family Interest

Mary's father was a wealthy merchant and trader. In those days, a beautiful daughter was a great boon, for the giving of a daughter in marriage was the way contracts and treaties were sealed between men of different families, tribes, and lands. Seeing the beauty of Mary, from early on he planned her marriage to a wealthy Jewish trader living in Babylon. He made certain Mary was well educated and learned proper etiquette, as well as all the crafts of a good wife and everything that would be pleasing to a powerful and wealthy man. Although, indeed, he knew he would have to provide a dowry, he also knew it was an investment that would return to him a hundredfold or more.

Mary's mother was quite pleased to see the attention showered on her daughter and all the preparations for her eventual marriage to a great man. She believed it was all the best for her daughter and would bring her happiness, because wealth and marriage meant these things to her mother. It was the purpose and meaning of life in her eyes. Besides, in those days, unless born among royalty of gentile nations, it was the best a woman could hope for, and it was her mother's hope for Mary. Mary's father had little love for his daughter; he was preoccupied with his own interests. However, Mary's mother loved her and wished the best for her, knowing all along that Mary was a special child, though never really understanding her daughter. Thus, Mary's mother labored with the same aim as Mary's father, although with a different intention.

The Inner Conflict of the Bride

From her early youth, Mary Magdalene dreamed luminous dreams and beheld divine visions. The spirits of prophets and holy angels came in dreams and visions to her, and they would teach her and show her secret things. Often, she dreamed of her Beloved and she was deeply in love with the Beloved who appeared in her dreams. She never spoke of these things to her father, but she did speak of them to her mother when she was little. When her mother would hear of the things Mary saw and heard, she discouraged her from speaking about them or believing in them.

Quite naturally, as Mary grew, an inner conflict ensued. It was as though she had two lives, one in the spiritual world and the other in the material world, and the two did not meet but were opposed to one another. In the depths of her being she was pulled one way; on the surface she was pulled another. In her heart she knew what was right and true. Yet, life dragged her along another way than that to which her soul was inclined. As one year passed into another, the inner conflict grew within her, until truly it was a torment in her soul. Not knowing what to do and without a spiritual mentor or close friend with knowledge of such things, eventually, when the pain became too great, she gave in and let go of the dreams of her youth and the desire of her holy soul.

The archons, of course, had a large hand in this, for with her great beauty and charm she could get almost anything in the world she desired. Nothing of the world was refused to her. In fact, her power over others, especially men, became somewhat intoxicating, and with the passage of time, even the thought of worldly wealth and power became desirable to her. With great skill, the archons wove the web to ensnare and trap the Holy Bride, and truth be told, they were nearly successful in their plot.

The Journey into Babylon

When Mary came of age, her father made arrangements for her and her handmaid, along with a dowry, to travel by caravan to Babylon, where the wealthy Jewish merchant lived to whom she had been promised in marriage. It was a painful departure, for it was then that, truly, she left her dreams behind and perhaps departed from her soul. Nevertheless, there was also excitement in Mary and great expectation. She had heard of the awesome splendor of Babylon and the adventure of travel thrilled her, as it often does with young people. A new life lay ahead of her, perhaps far richer. Thus the pain of her departure was tempered with the enthusiasm of the adventure.

The caravan was to proceed by way of Damascus and then on into the heart of Babylon. On the road going out of Damascus, the caravan was beset by a large band of robbers who swiftly overtook it. These roads were notorious for bandits and were the known haunts of demons. Even though on guard, the caravan was at their mercy. The robbers killed all of the men. While they plundered the caravan, they raped Mary, her handmaid, and the other women who were with them. It was as though the jaws of hell opened to consume the caravan and demons were loosed upon Mary and the women to defile them and crush their souls.

It is said that, when Magdalene was being raped, Lilith, the Dark Sophia, was watching and that she saw the Light in Mary and was attracted to it. Now Lilith has no love of men because of her plight with Adam before the beginning of time, and she has no love of submissive women because of her jealousy of Eve who took her place with Adam.

In Mary, she saw something else, something that fascinated her, and seeing the evil and violence of the men, she was inclined toward Mary and felt for her. Thus, Lilith waited until evening. Once the darkness of night came, it is said she entered into Mary Magdalene and all of her rage and brooding darkness entered with her. Really, it is only to be expected, for what transpires in the experience of a woman being raped?

Now at the moment Lilith entered into Mary, the robber who was raping Mary was the leader of the horde, and he intended to take her for himself. Instead, with her magic power, Lilith slew him, so that shortly thereafter he fell dead. The bandits did not associate this with Magdalene. They took her, along with all of the women, and sold her into slavery in Babylon.

Thus it has been said that Eve and Lilith were joined in St. Mary of Magdal, the Bright and Dark Sophia, although it was Lilith who held dominion while Our Lady was in exile in Babylon. Although perchance Lilith led her into great darkness, so also she served to preserve her life, and as it came to pass, she facilitated Mary's restoration to her inmost heart's desire. All of this is a great mystery that can only be discerned inwardly! Yet we suspect many women will innately understand, for many have fallen under the dominion of the male demiurge and survived the dire straits only through the grace of Lilith.

The Slavery of Prostitution

It was not by choice that Mary fell into prostitution. Being purchased as a slave in Babylon, the man who bought her turned her out as a whore. She thought of attempting to escape, but she no longer had any place to go and no means of travel. She considered taking her own life, but there was a rage and desire for vengeance in her that would not allow it—the influence of Lilatu,[12] no doubt. Then, as though by inspiration, she noticed the reaction to her charms by wealthy and powerful men. She began to pay special attention to the most wealthy and powerful who purchased time with her. It was not long before she enticed one of them to buy her freedom, thinking to take her as his wife on account of her great beauty. Once she had her freedom and was bought a residence in the city of Babylon, she would not marry him. Instead, she courted the attention of the most wealthy and powerful men to support herself and to gather a treasury and power to herself. There really was nothing else she could do at the time, and a deep desire for vengeance fueled the zeal for her activities. When she acquired the opportunity and ability to do so, she conspired to have the man killed who had bought her as a slave and made her a prostitute.

Much to her surprise, the death of her oppressor brought her no relief or satisfaction. The rage, hatred, and darkness remained in her, and the pit of emptiness did not depart from her. It is this that attracted seven demons to her, from whom she gained certain magic powers related to enchantments. Although she courted men, in truth she despised them, and inwardly she loathed herself as well. From one gradation to another, she fell into an ever-greater darkness and void, as though passing through the seven abodes of Gehenna to the deepest pit of pure ice. So it was that her heart was hardened and she was exiled from her holy soul. Inwardly, she was slain and left in great torment. It was as though she was an empty shell filled only by chaos and void, akin to the primeval earth at the outset of the entirety.[13] The plot of the demiurgos and archons had come to fruition, only they never suspected Lilatu would become involved and serve to act against them.

Lilith and the Archons

It is not surprising that Lilith would act against the demiurgos and archons, for as is reflected by male domination in the world, the demiurgos is male and so also are the majority of the archons. Merely consider the nature of pride and arrogance, or lust and greed, or anger and hate, these powers of war and conquest. Although the heart of Sophian Nigrans[14] emanates as Naamah, the Queen of Demons, and her inmost dark essence emanates as Iggaret, the Hag of Chaos, nevertheless Sophia Nigrans is not among the dark and hostile forces nor is she counted among the archons. She seeks to redress the balance in the play of cosmic forces. So it is said that, when the Shekinah is in exile, she is the Divine Consort of the Most High, for she seeks to restore the union of the Father and Mother and to transcend male and female, as was her state in Adam Ha-Rishon at the outset. Thus, entering into Mary, Lilatu wove her web to snare the demiurgos and archons and to cast down male domination! If you can glimpse the inner and secret meaning of this, you will be called wise. Is she not the Dark Wisdom of God through which rebirth in the Spirit comes to pass?

The Return of the Bride from Her Exile

When Mary Magdalene was in the depths of darkness, her soul appearing slain under the dominion of the demiurgos and archons, memories of the dreams and visions of her youth returned to her and the Divine spark within the inmost recesses of her heart ignited, as light entered in. At first, it brought her no comfort, but seemed more like taunting and torment. The demons that were with her struggled against the Light and did everything in their power to overcome it. Nevertheless, Mary began to turn toward the Light and to kindle the holy spark of her soul. She strove against the demons and all of the darkness that was in her, repenting of the darkness and calling out to the Mother, to Divine Grace.

The Spirit of Yaweh answered Mary and empowered her. She withdrew from whoredom and began to use her wealth and power to render assistance to the poor in Babylon. It is said that she bought the freedom of many female slaves and restored them to life, and that in the midst of Babylon, a city of archons worshipped as gods and goddesses, she worshipped the Alien God[15] whose name was El Elyon, God Most High. She knew God as her Father and her Mother, and the Spirit of God was with her. After some time, the Lord sent a man of God to call her in from her exile. Some say it was a holy man who came to her; others say it was the angel of John the Baptist. In any case, the messenger came and she received him. He said to Mary, "In your youth you dreamed dreams and saw visions, and the Spirit of the Lord spoke in you. Listen and hear the word of the Lord, and remember the path of your holy soul and the image of your Beloved. The Lord calls you in from your exile, that you might follow your dreams and seek your Beloved. Pass now from darkness into Light, and from death into life. Your father is dead, and your Father in heaven calls you to return to the holy land. There seek out your Beloved, the Anointed, and be received by the Mother Spirit."

That very day, St. Mary Magdalene made arrangements for her journey back to the holy land, finding a caravan that was to depart the next day. She took a moderate amount of her wealth and gave the remainder to the poor. At dawn she set out, cleaving in her heart to the Spirit of Yahweh and Shekinah. This was the beginning of the Bride's redemption, and Lilith with her.

Twin Souls

There was one supernal soul in Lord Yeshua and St. Mary Magdalene, he the male and she the female emanation of one soul of Light. Hence, it is said that they were soul mates. So it is with every supernal soul, for all human souls were in the supernal Human Being. Thus, when the Holy One divided the Human One into male and female, all holy souls were also divided into male and female counterparts, which are destined to meet and unite with one another in the cycles of transmigration.

Soul mates, therefore, have an intimate secret connection, and so it was between Yeshua and Mary. Even before meeting, they beheld one another in dreams and visions and were deeply connected. Thus, whatever happened for one also happened for the other, to some degree. So long as Mary was in exile, Yeshua's holy soul was not fully in his body. It came into his body on the day the Spirit of Yahweh called her in from exile, for on that very day Yeshua was baptized by John in the Jordan River and the Spirit of the Messiah entered into him.

We all know that the Spirit drove Yeshua into the wilderness of the desert to be tempted by Satan. At the same time, Mary was traveling in a caravan through the desert as she made her way back to the holy land. She, too, struggled with Satan and the seven demons that were with her. At night, the wrestling became most severe. They tormented her all that way, and the nearer to the holy land she came, the greater the temptation and torment they inflicted upon her. Never-

theless, she cleaved to the Spirit of Truth[16] and believed in the power
of her Beloved to heal her. She did not turn away from the Lord.

It is said that St. Mary Magdalene entered into the holy land on
the very day when Lord Yeshua performed his first wonder-working
act at the wedding feast in Cana, where he turned water into wine as
a prophecy of her return.[17] The masters of the tradition teach that in
the story of this first wonder are secrets of the love-play of the Holy
Bride and Bridegroom, Our Lady and Our Lord.

Pure Emanation

Among the masters of the tradition there has always been a debate,
for some say Yeshua and Mary were a holy man and woman into
whom the Soul of the Messiah entered, but others say they were pure
emanations and not flesh and blood as ordinary human beings. In
truth, it is a great mystery, and perhaps the truth lies in between. Nevertheless, they appeared among us, and lived and moved among us,
and they brought forth the Supernal Light into the world. To this
very day, they remain with us and appear to the elect who seek their
acquaintance.

Among those who speak of pure emanations, it is said that Yeshua
was born of the Virgin Mother, but that Mary was a spontaneous emanation, having neither father nor mother in this world. She merely
entered and appeared when it was time to take up the sacred dance
with the Lord, as though the light and fire of heaven came down to
appear as a holy woman—the Shekinah Consort of the Anointed.

Others say that she is the Holy Spirit and that when Yeshua returned from the wilderness of the desert, he appeared walking hand in
hand with her as he came among the people, and that she was the display of all the wonders he performed and the supernal fire that
poured out at the Pentecost.

Yet others have said she emanated from within the Great Master, as
the emanation of the Sacred Heart, when he turned water into wine
at the wedding feast; and thus, in truth, it was their own wedding
feast that was celebrated on that holy day.

Then there are those who say that, all the while, Our Lord and Lady appeared only in the visionary dimension to those who had eyes to see and ears to hear the coming into being of the Supernal Human One among us—that they are the vision of our soul of Light emerging through the matrix of the material dimension. Those who are wise say that there is truth to all of these views; for to anyone who might gaze upon them, Yeshua and Mary are more than they appear to be.

Now, if Our Lady was a pure emanation, then she was never a prostitute, but ever pure; and her true name is Sophia, or Hokmah in Hebrew. She is the Mother come down to live and move among us, even as Our Lord is the image of the Living Father revealed to us. If she is the emanation of the Divine Mother, Elohim,[18] then she is also the emanation of the Soul of the World whom the Lord embraced and raised up in the resurrection and ascension. It is for this reason that it is she who greeted the Risen Savior on the Day of Be-With-Us. Anyone who seeks the acquaintance of Our Lord and Lady of Initiation must look within him or herself, for there is where all acquaintance is.

Eve and the Serpent

Eve received knowledge, understanding, and wisdom from the serpent. She gave it to Adam. He received it through her, and thus the journey of the descent of human souls into the world began. Knowledge, understanding, and wisdom come by way of involution into the material dimension, through which the activation and evolution of the soul transpires. When there were bodies fit to receive human souls, human souls entered into them. This was the beginning of human beings on earth, all by way of evolution.

What did the serpent give to the Mother of Life? He gave the gift of a fiery intelligence, which was the fruit of the Tree of Knowledge of Good and Evil; for only when souls shine with the Light of the Spiritual Sun is it right that they should partake of the fruit of the Tree of Life and enter the Supernal Abode.

It has been said that Eve led Adam into death, and this is true; but it is written, "Unless a grain of wheat falls into the earth and dies, it shall in no wise bear forth good fruit." So, in truth, the Mother of Life sought to bring good fruit through the generations of Adam, the human being, and she is Sophia at play in creation, all according to the conception in the mind of God who spoke the Living Word. This good fruit is the Christos, the Light-presence.

Eve led the descent, and she became St. Mary Magdalene to complete the transmission of gnosis, understanding, and wisdom. Thus, she went down into the depths of darkness and rose up, opening the way for the Savior to go down and rise up as the Living Yeshua. Just as Eve gave knowledge, understanding, and wisdom to Adam, so was St. Mary Magdalene the Divine Muse of Our Lord.

Some might object and say, "Is not the serpent who spoke to Eve Satan, the great adversary?" Indeed! But is not adversity essential in the evolution to the Highest of Life? When the Highest of Life is attained, is not all adversity redeemed? It is for this reason that, just as St. Mary Magdalene passed down into great darkness and was redeemed, so also the masters of the tradition say that, in the End-of-Days, the great adversary will also be redeemed. Thus it has been said, "Eve is redeemed in Lady Mary and the serpent is redeemed in Lord Yeshua." Look and see! The Risen Savior appeared first to Lady Mary, and then, as Eve, she gave also to the sons of Adam!

Sun and Moon

Everything below is also found above, for all things are founded upon their supernal and holy pattern. Thus, just as there is a sun and moon below, so there is a sun and moon above, though of another order entirely. Yeshua was like a ray of the Spiritual Sun manifest in human form and Magdalene was like a beam of the Spiritual Moon, both the emanation of Luminous and Holy Being.

The lunar cycle begins with the darkness of the new moon and then grows bright at the time of the full moon. In the same way, Mary begins in darkness and then waxes bright as she draws near to Yeshua, the Spiritual Sun. This is not to say that she has no light of her own or that she is not co-equal with him. This is a metaphor that reflects several truths of the mystery and proves a worthy contemplation. She herself said, "He is the sun and I am the moon, and I am that space in which the Light shines."

Now we may say this: It is through Our Lady that we receive the Light of Our Lord, and it is she who stirs the Sea of the Divine Life.

The Mystery

Truth be told, the early life of the Bride is a complete mystery; for the beginning of her life is shrouded in secrecy and thick darkness. It truly begins when she meets Lord Yeshua and the light of her holy soul bursts forth from within her. It is just the same with the wisdom nature in us. It, too, is hidden until the Light-presence emerges to reveal our true origin. It is the same with all of us when we discover the Living Yeshua within us. On that day, our life begins!

So the masters of the tradition say that the story of Our Lady is our story, as surely as the story of womanhood is the story of life.

The Holy Bride, St. Mary Magdalene, reveals herself to everyone willing to receive her, and she is an endless divine mystery of Life-power.

Notes

1. Hebrew pronunciation of Sabbath.

2. Literally, "righteous ones."

3. A title of the Holy Shekinah.

4. Titles of the Upper and Lower Shekinah; hence the Divine Presence and Power above and below.

5. Personification of the Bright and Dark aspects of Sophia.

6. A term for the name Yahweh.

7. A term for the World of Supernal Light; parallel to the Gnostic term bridal chamber.

8. A noted disciple of St. Mary Magdalene, sharing this name with two others: Salome the Maiden and Salome the Elder.

9. Literally, "rulers," which in Christian Gnostic teachings represent cosmic or spiritual forces bound to cosmic ignorance; hence the demiurge of Gnosticism.

10. Literally, "false god" or "false creator," the personification of cosmic ignorance or falsehood in Gnostic Christianity.

11. The personification of dark and hostile forces in Gnostic Christianity, typically distinct from the demiurgos and archons that are spoken of as admixed.

14. Another name of Lilith.

13. A gnostic term for the matrix of creation.

14. Literally, "Black Sophia" or "Dark Sophia."

15. A term often used for God in Gnosticism.

16. A common term for the Holy Spirit or Mother Spirit.

17. Gospel of St. John 2:1–11.

18. The divine name associated with the Mother, which is a feminine noun and masculine plural, implying the One and Many or Oneness and Multiplicity.

CYCLE 3

THE UNION OF THE
BRIDE AND YESHUA

First Glance

Once St. Mary Magdalene had returned to the holy land, straightaway she set out to find the Anointed. The Holy Spirit led her to him, and Mary found him teaching a large crowd of people. The people were gathered all around him, seated on the ground. His disciples were closest to him, and he stood in their midst while he spoke. Mary sat down, hiding herself at the outskirts of the circle. She listened intently to the Lord as he spoke. His voice was as the cooing of a dove to her. Yet his words were like thunder and burned her to the core. It was a great beauty and great danger to listen to him, and she could sense something awesome about to transpire. She broke out in a sweat and trembled. Just then, he met her gaze. It was just a glance and a subtle smile, yet energy and vibration filled her whole body. It was electrical and she had never felt anything like it. She looked at her hands and touched her face in amazement. She was taken up in awe, wonder, and the deepest love.

Years later, she would tell of hearing his voice speaking inwardly, within her own mind, though she never shared with anyone what he said to her. She could not hear what he was saying outwardly any longer, only what he spoke within her. She sat completely astonished, and then her mind and heart fell into a deep clarity and silence. The Lord did not glance at her again as he taught the people. When he finished speaking, he charged his disciples to send the people away and asked two of his disciples to bring Mary to him. He went ahead and Thomas accompanied him. He went out into the wilderness to the Jordan River and waited. Thomas inquired of Yeshua, saying, "Lord, what does this woman have to do with you?" Jesus said to Thomas, "When you know who I am, you will know who she is, and you will understand." It was evening when the disciples brought Magdalene to him and he rose to greet her. It was then that the seven demons were cast out of her.

The Witness of the Matchmaker

A matchmaker witnessed the exchange of glance between the Lord and Mary, and she knew in that instant that they were in love and it was destined for them to be together. More than this, to her astonishment, she saw a light-image come out of the Lord and a light-image come out of Mary, and the two merged completely together. She said of this light-image, "I dared not gaze at it, because it was blinding. Flashing fire was coming out of it, and I feared for my life. It was too great a holiness." Because of what she had seen, she did not tell anyone. She only spoke of it to the women disciples of the Lord sometime after Yeshua and Mary were husband and wife.

When it came to pass many years later and the matchmaker died, when her soul passed through the domains of the archons and the celestial abodes, no guardian would challenge her. Having beheld the image of the Second Adam, the glory of the image was upon her for all to see. As it is known among initiates, one cannot see something that one does not become.

The Exorcism of the Bride

When Lady Mary was brought to the Lord by the two disciples he charged to bring her, he was seated with Thomas by a fire near at the edge of the holy river. He and Thomas were meditating together, gazing into the fire as the Lord taught many to do. As Mary drew near, he looked up at her and rose to greet her. As he laid his hands upon her, he said, "Out!" Immediately, seven demons were flung out of her and were cast into the fire. The fire exploded into a great blaze and Thomas was startled, because all the while he was entranced, beholding visions of the heavens in the flames. He yelled out, "Heaven became hell!" While holding his gaze upon Magdalene, the Lord said to him, "Yes,

Thomas, the same spirit appears as these, as light and fire, but the True Light is beyond them." Then he chose Thomas and Philip and said to them, "Baptize this woman, so that she should be received among us." So the disciples baptized St. Mary Magdalene and she was liberated from her bondage. Then the Lord took Mary by the hand, saying, "Come, follow me," and he took her out into the wilderness alone.

The Seven Demons and Seven Angels

The names of the seven demons are well known and it is best we do not speak them. To speak the name of a spirit is to conjure it, and only a fool or an evil person would knowingly invoke demons. How these came to be in the Bride is quite simple. When she was in Babylon, her soul passed in descent through Hades and the seven abodes of Gehenna, even into the darkest pit. There, her soul was crucified by that dark power whose name is dreadful. In each abode of Gehenna, she left sparks of her soul behind, until only the faintest spark was left to glimmer. From each dark and hostile abode, a demon was attached to her, to bind her soul and cause her anguish.

Thus, when the Lord exorcised the seven demons, he also gathered up the sparks of Mary's soul from the abodes of Gehenna, restoring her soul to her completely. Then he invoked her supernal soul, so that nothing in the heavens, on earth, or of Gehenna should ever have power over her again.

It is said that, when the Lord banished the seven demons, he then established seven angels in their place. These were the seven archangels who walked with the Lord on earth: Tzaphkiel, Tzadkiel, Kamael, Raphael, Uriel, Michael, and Gabriel. Once Our Lord and Lady were joined, it is said that Metatron and Sandalfon walked with them too. Of course, the angel of Sophia walked with Lady Mary also; thus Ratziel was with them as well. There is no doubt of the Pleroma[1] of Light with Our Lady and Our Lord.

Yeshua and Mary in the Wilderness

When Yeshua took Mary out into the wilderness, he led her to a place of power that was known as holy by the mystics of the time. It was the time of the full moon and the moon shone brightly in the night sky. Without any words passing between them, they sat together in prayer and meditation, keeping vigil through the night. Many righteous spirits and angels gathered in the subtle dimensions around them, for they wished to worship with the Bride and Bridegroom, and sought to witness what was about to transpire.

It was the season when the bright morning star heralds the passage of the sun in the gate of the east. As the morning star arose, Mary spoke, saying, "My Lord, why have you brought me out here? Why do you touch an unclean woman, for you are a holy man and it is forbidden by the law?" Yeshua said, "Woman, I am the fulfillment of the law. The purpose of the law is to bind the demiurgos and archons and to destroy the hold of the devil, not to bind the soul of the human one. I have brought you here because you shall be my bride and consort, and I shall be your Lord and husband. In you, the Soul of the World shall be redeemed." Mary said, "I know you are my Beloved, but how can this be? You do not understand who I have become, that I am unclean and defiled, so that no righteous man can take me as his wife." Yeshua said to her, "The woman of whom you speak is not the woman who sits with me now. You speak of the dead, but you are among the living. Yesterday no longer exists, tomorrow has not yet come to pass. The only existence is today, and those who are alive today are the living ones. My Beloved, I receive you as you are and you are as you were before you were born and as you forever shall be, the illumination and glory of this I Am."

When Mary heard these words, she burst into tears and said, "My Beloved, my Savior, my Soul, and my Truth—Adonai!" And they embraced and the Lord kissed her on her lips for the first time. We can only imagine the power of this moment, for, if with the first glance we hear of an intense exchange of sparks, then surely this set the world on fire! Indeed, it did, for when they had embraced, Mary said to Yeshua, "My Lord, you know the Way. Please teach me the Way, so that I might walk with you in the Light and abide always in the

Truth." Yeshua said to her, "Most Beloved, it shall come to pass as you have spoken it. The eve of the Shabbat approaches, and when the Shabbat passes between us, then I will give what you ask of me and you shall become the Wisdom treasury of the kingdom."

On the morning of the first day of the week, the Master began teaching Mary the Way. Lord Yeshua instructed her in the Gospel of Truth, and imparted to her the outer, inner, and secret Gospel. He instructed her in the mysteries of the Fifty Gates of Understanding, including that most Holy Gate even Moses was unable to comprehend; he taught her of the Seventy Gates of Wisdom and the Forty Gates of the Supernal Crown. He taught her the Way of the Name and all unifications, and the mysteries of baptism of fire and Spirit, supernal chrism, the wedding feast of Melchizedek, the rite of ransom, and the bridal chamber.

When the Lord completed all of these teachings, he invoked the Great Angel of the Shekinah as a holy sanctuary, and in secret he spoke of the many ways the soul might instantly attain the Divine rapture of unification with God. He did this so that neither angel nor spirit might hear these inmost secret teachings which God ordained that the Anointed should teach only to human beings.

This transpired for six days, and on the seventh day, they celebrated the Shabbat together. When the Shabbat came to an end, the Lord returned to his disciples who were waiting for him where he had left them, by the River Jordan. He announced to them that Mary was to become his wife and gave them instructions for the preparation of the wedding feast. Needless to say, many of the male disciples were shocked by this, but they did not question him about it at that time. There was a presence about him they had not seen before, which struck them with silence.

Eve and Lilith

In the beginning, Eve and Lilith were joined together, the image of the Supernal Woman, a pure emanation. Some say that Adam was overwhelmed by the glory and grace of the perfect woman. Thus, her power and luminosity was reduced, Lilith being divided from Eve, and Adam received the submissive woman.

Others say that Lilith, alone, was Adam's first wife, but that she was not submissive enough. When they made love, Adam always demanded to be on top. Therefore, Lilith left him, finding the lack of equality unacceptable. Lilith was a pure supernal emanation, but Eve was created to replace her.

In any case, Lilith and Eve were divided, and the glory of womanhood was incomplete. On account of this, there was strife between Eve and Lilith, and Lilith stalked the sons of Adam born of Eve. Cain and Abel fell by way of Lilith's enchantments, but because of this, the Great Seth arose.

Now, Eve and Lilith were reunited in Lady Mary, and she was a whole woman. When the Lord banished the seven demons from Magdalene, he did not banish Lilith. Rather, receiving the Holy Bride, he redeemed Lilith and Eve, and in Lady Mary, womanhood was restored to its rightful place, for in her was the Divine fullness of the Supernal Woman.

Yeshua was called the Son of Adam, which is to say the son of the human one, and the fullness of the Great Seth was in him, the image and likeness of the Supernal Man. Thus, united with the Holy Bride, who is the embodiment of the Supernal Woman, he and she became the Second Adam, exalted above the First Adam who was incomplete. Our Lord was not overwhelmed by the fullness of true womanhood. Therefore, in the Holy Bride he was made whole and complete, and in the Bridegroom she was fulfilled and made perfect. In the Groom and Bride, a new and supernal humanity was created, and all who receive the Light-transmission are of the new race of the Second Adam.

The Mystical Union of Our Lord and Our Lady

The wedding of Our Lord and Our Lady took place in the wilderness, near the River Jordan where John the Baptist preached. John presided over the ceremony, as was fitting, for he was the Tzaddik of the Messiah and his angel called the Bride in from her exile. The disciples of the Lord and the disciples of John were in attendance. Mother Mary and the brothers of the Lord were also there. A glorious wedding canopy was erected, along with tents for the celebration. Good food and wine and musicians were brought out. Truly, it was a great and holy wedding feast, and there was celebration on earth and in heaven.

Now in the spaces in between and in the abodes of Gehenna, there was fear and trembling. It was the wedding of Christ the Logos and Christ the Sophia, and the plots of the demiurgos and Satan had, as it were, unraveled and failed. The Pleroma of Supernal Light had entered in and the Supernal Image of the Most High was manifest among humankind. When the Lord crushed the cup under his foot and Mazzal Tov[2] was proclaimed, it was good news for the world, for so also were the dominion of the demiurgos and the husks of darkness[3] shattered. It was the beginning of the end.

When Lord Yeshua and Lady Mary were united, John beheld light and fire pour down upon them and a heavenly voice said, "Behold, the Lamb of God and New Jerusalem come down; the perfection of all creation. It is good, it is very good." Then the spirit of the prophets broke out in the assembly and the Holy Spirit was upon them, so that men and women spoke prophecies and the wedding feast became a worship of God in Spirit and Truth, a worshipping in the presence of Yahweh.

The wedding of the Lord and the Holy Bride was the union of a priest-king and priestess-queen according to the order of Melchizedek, and in Our Lord and Our Lady is the image of the high priest, male and female joined in one Body of Light, the Spiritual Sun. That night, the sun shone at midnight and all who were present were anointed with the Supernal Light of God.

The Invocation of the Holy Bride

The Spirit of Yahweh called the Bride in from her exile, but it was Mother Wisdom at the wedding feast in Cana of Galilee who invoked the union of the Son and Daughter. At the wedding feast, Mother Sophia said to her son, "Look, my son, it is time to invoke your bride. For there is no wine in the circle and you are, as yet, incomplete without her. It is written, 'Yahweh Elohim created the Human One, male and female, in the image of Elohim and likeness of Yahweh.' As the Son of the Human One, you must also be male and female, lest the image and likeness of the Living Father remain incomplete. It is for the sake of the Bride Sophia that you have come into the world, so that she might be redeemed, and in her the Soul of the World might be redeemed."

The Lord said to the Mother, "Woman, what concern is it to us if there is wine or no wine? My time has not yet come." Mother Sophia responded, saying, "Do we not bless Adonai[4] who brings forth the fruit of the vine from the earth, which makes glad the hearts of human beings? Do we not receive in order to give? If not now, then when shall your time come?" Then she said to the angels of God, "Do whatever he tells you to do."

What transpires below also transpires above; the stirring below invokes a stirring above. When the Lord commanded the servants at the wedding feast to fill six stone jars with water, angels in heaven gathered six Light-emanations and filled them with Supernal Grace. When the water in the stone jars was transformed into wine, Supernal Grace in the Light-emanations became the Holy Fire of the Bride and all of the blessing power of the Supernal Abode poured out upon the earth. It was the invocation of the Holy Bride, initiated by Mother Wisdom and spoken by the Son of the Human One. At the wedding feast of Our Lady and Our Lord, the invocation was fulfilled and the Bride was received.

The Bridal Chamber

When Yeshua and Mary entered into the tent, which was the bridal chamber, God and the Shekinah entered into the supernal tent, which is the bridal chamber above. Uniting male and female below, the Father and Mother were united above, and Supernal Grace poured forth upon the world. It is forbidden to speak of what transpires in the bridal chamber. But we can say this: There was Light upon Light and Fire consuming Fire, so that, in the bridal chamber, a new heaven and new earth were conceived. The joy of Our Lord and Our Lady is the joy of the whole world. On that night, the Original Blessing was restored. Since that holy night the World of Supernal Light has remained within and all around us, only there are few who have eyes to see it.

The Companion of the Lord

Three holy women always walked with the Lord: Mary, the Holy Mother; Mary, the Old Wise Woman; and St. Mary Magdalene, the Maiden of Light. Now their proper name in Hebrew is Miriam. They are the three faces of True Womanhood and the Divine Mother, so that, as well as the image of the Living Father, the image of the Divine Mother was always with him. In Mary Magdalene, he was joined to the Divine Mother as the Living Father to the Holy Shekinah, for she was his wife and consort.

St. Mary Magdalene never left the side of the Lord from the day of their union until the night of the Passion. She ate with him and slept with him. She laughed with him and cried with him, and she went everywhere with him. She was the only disciple who accompanied him on his spiritual retreats and kept vigils of prayer and meditation with him. Because he kissed her often on the mouth in public, it was an embarrassment to the male disciples. Because he gave her secret teachings that he spoke to no other disciple, many of the men disciples were jealous of her. At dinners and festivals in the homes of believers, they danced together and made merry. It was not uncommon for them to walk arm in arm. The Lord said of her, "She is my very self and soul in woman's form. I am she and she is what I am," though few were able to listen and hear this. Even to this day, few believe that Christ can come in a woman's form and few have received Our Lady, the Holy Bride.

Lord Yeshua taught men and women alike, and Lady Mary was his inmost secret disciple, along with her twin, St. Lazarus.[5] At night, in private when they were alone, he disclosed every mystery to her and taught her every secret thing. She taught and initiated the women and any men who would receive her. She co-preached the Gospel of Truth with Lord Yeshua and performed all manner of wonders, for she was coequal and co-enlightened with him. He is Christ the Logos and she is Christ the Sophia. Together, they are the Second Adam, the seed of supernal humanity.

Many can accept she was a close disciple, some can accept she was the wife and consort of the Lord, but few are they who accept her as the female embodiment of the Christos. These latter are called Sophians, for they have gnosis of Logos and Sophia. Thus, among us, there are both men and women who are elders and tau—apostles of Light.

If an ordinary man and woman become one flesh in marriage, then a man and woman of Light become one holy soul. So it is with Our Lady and Our Lord; they embody the Soul of the Messiah.

The Divine Muse

It was a great blessing that the Holy Mother inspired the Lord to invoke the Bride, for St. Mary Magdalene is the Divine muse of the Gospel of Truth. It is she who inspired the Lord to impart the outer, inner, and secret teachings of the Gospel. Apart from her, he would not have given the inner and secret initiations. It was to her that he spoke of the deep mysteries, all in a constant courtship and love-play. She knew how to ask questions when other disciples were present, so that, answering her, all were blessed with secret Wisdom.

Few could conceive of such sublime and powerful passion as occurred between Our Lord and Our Lady. Through their passion, the whole world has been set ablaze. In his passion for Our Lady, Our Lord kindled the flames until they poured forth upon the entire assembly, making the true and Gnostic church like unto the Holy Fire of the Bride—on fire with the Spirit of Yahweh. Truly, without her, we would only have the outer Gospel, as in the outer and unspiritual church, and dead letters devoid of the life of the Holy Spirit.

The Lord loved Mary Magdalene so deeply that he poured himself into her, and thus he said to the male disciples who complained that he taught a woman, "I shall make her male, like unto you males." Likewise, when they complained he loved her more than all his disciples, he said to them, "Give thanks I love her as I do, for because of her you also receive. And if you are wise, you will inquire of yourselves why I love her more than I love you." Indeed! He loved her because she saw him and knew him and received the anointing he received, for she was his soul mate.

Soul Mates

Many speak of meeting their soul mate, but they do not know what they are saying. When soul mates meet, there is light and fire between them, and they give birth to something new in the world and are a blessing on the world. The nature of the meeting and union of soul mates is that humanity is uplifted through their love-play. It truly is no trivial matter, as we see in the mystical union of Our Lady and Our Lord. Their love was not their own, nor was it isolated to them, but the whole world has been changed by it. Soul mates are divine consorts and partners in the great work. Joined together, they fulfill the mission of the Supernal Soul they share. By this, we know when soul mates meet and unite—they are a Light in the world, as Our Lady and Lord are Light. In this way, we understand the divine passion that transpired between them and a secret mystery of salvation.

The Holy Staff of the Lord

There is a strange legend told of the Lord and the Bride. It is said that the Lord had a holy staff with the Great Name of God engraved upon it and that its shape was that of a serpent. He carried it with him everywhere he went, up until the time of the Passion and his arrest. When he spoke to the multitudes, the staff looked like an ordinary staff. When he taught his disciples in private, it often transformed into a serpent that would coil up near him. Sometimes, when the Lord wished to initiate a disciple, the staff, transformed into the serpent, would go to the disciple and bite him, injecting gnosis and power. At some point, every new disciple was put to the test in this way, and many fled from the Good Serpent.

The holy staff would become other things as well. It would become the power of fire or ice and often shone with brilliant light. Once it transformed into a phoenix bird and flew into heaven to fetch a star-crown jewel of Wisdom. On more than one occasion it became a thunderbolt in the Lord's hands, and other times, a great ray of light. Sometimes, it changed into an archangel or some other luminous being. Once when he was preaching in a town and the people became hostile toward Our Lady, he hid her in it and made himself invisible, escaping in this way, for the full power of the Holy Shekinah was in his staff.

In truth, it was Our Lady who was his Shekinah consort and holy staff of power. The Great Name burned upon her brow, the milk and honey of the Tree of Life flowed through her, and she was as the living temple in which the Lord dwelt. In this, deep things are spoken for those who might understand.

The Mysteries of the Arayot

The Lord knew the mysteries of the Arayot[6] and practiced them with St. Mary Magdalene. These are the mysteries of a man embracing a woman as the physical embodiment of the Shekinah of God and the woman embracing the man as the physical embodiment of Yahweh. It was in this way that they made love. Thus, in their love, they played among the Light-emanations and brought down the everflowing and radiant holy breath for all to receive. Some have said that the great wonders that transpired were on account of this, though surely it was only part of the mystery of the great wonder-working power in Our Lord and Our Lady.

Now among the things those skilled in the Arayot are able to do is to conceive a child and draw down a holy soul of a very high grade. One can only imagine the loftiness of the holy soul that Yeshua and Mary brought into the world, for it is said that their son, St. Michael, was conceived in this way.

Many wonders were seen in the nights that Yeshua and Mary embraced in this way, but these are improper to speak about, as they belong between Our Lady and Our Lord.

If an elder[7] or tau[8] is to teach these mysteries, he or she can only speak them in the presence of two disciples, and only where there is love and a covenant rightly established. Yet it is said that Mary Magdalene taught these mysteries to many women disciples and that they, in turn, instructed their husbands.

The Dance of the Bride

Lady Mary loved to dance for the Lord and for the disciples. Her dance would draw souls into ecstasy and beatific visions. Light and fire would come from her body, and with her dance she would compel spirits. Whatever she desired, spirits would do. The spirits of saints and angels would dance with her in the subtle air, and the Shekinah would rest upon her so that blessings and grace poured out. Oftentimes, the Lord would take up the dance with her, and many amazing wonders transpired in this way. It was a dance of perfect devekut.[9] Yet just as often, the Lord would sit perfectly still in the center, abiding in prayer and chant and holy meditation. She would dance a circle around him, extending the light and glory of the Anointed.

If anyone who had any unclean or evil spirit entered when Our Lady was dancing, the dark spirit would be driven out of them. If any were ill, they would be healed. Many experienced states of divine illumination while she danced, worshipping her Beloved and the Holy One of Being.

When she wished to dance alone, no one would rise to join her, but all sat entranced and enchanted by her dancing. Yet, when she wished others to join in, her dance would become intoxicating, so that no one could remain still. The energy of her dance would pass like a wildfire to all who were present, and all manner of prayers were answered when she danced.

Indeed! She would become as the heavenly woman whom neither man nor angel could refuse. She prayed and invoked God the Mother often in this way. It was she who taught worship through dance to the young women of the circle, just as she taught them the courtly affairs of the royal path of the priestess-queen. For she was in every way the priestess-queen and Kallah Messiah,[10] and though she loved to dance, she also bore her regal bearing when sitting, as though enthroned. When she walked, she was the movement of perfect grace. She danced and sat and walked in great beauty and holiness. In every way, she was the worthy consort and partner of Our Lord.

Mysteries of the Moon

Our Lady taught and initiated many women disciples, and among the women there were many who grew wise. She taught all aspects of the Gospel, just as the Lord taught the Gospel, but she also taught all mysteries of the Gospel in womanhood. At the heart of her teachings of the Gospel in womanhood were the mysteries of the cycle of the moon known to women. When the cycle of the moon comes full circle with a woman, there is great power in her and she becomes more sensitive to the subtle air and spiritual world. Thus, Lady Mary taught the way of spiritual retreat and vision quest to women of the circle, following the cycles of the moon in their own bodies. She also taught them ways of prophecy and wonder-working as was once known to the prophetess Miriam.

When the women would retreat in this way, it was for the sake of the tikkune[11] of the world and restoration of true womanhood. Now these mysteries cannot be spoken openly, only in circle. Yet, we can say she taught women how to chant the Mother's names, how to sing heart-songs, how to celebrate in the Mother Spirit, and how to bring tikkune to the world of angels and the world of Light-emanations, as well as to this good earth and the human spirit.

Men and women alike received teachings and initiations from Yeshua and Mary, and no difference was made among them in the First Circle.[12] Women were considered clean and holy in their womanhood, and the taint of false doctrines inspired by the demiurge was purified. Here, we can mention the saying of the Lord when he gave his heart-advice to the Holy Bride. First, he said to her, "Seek to know nothing, and seek to understand nothing; do not seek to be anybody. In this way you will acquire the perfection of wisdom." Then he said to her, "The divine illumination of the Anointed is the same for men and women alike, and both men and women can equally attain it. Yet, when the Light-presence is embodied in a woman, she is a greater power for the good than the man who embodies it. So it shall be in the Second Coming—the great matrix of the supernal Light-presence shall manifest through true womanhood."

This is the hope of the Second Coming among Sophians.

The Virgin and the Whore

Now it has been said that the Mother was the virgin and that the Bride was the whore, and both were called "Mary." Why should the Mother be called a Virgin and the Bride called a whore? Because Mother Sophia is concealed and Bride Sophia is revealed. Anyone who seeks to know the Holy Bride will know her, but no one shall know the Mother, save the Daughter.

There is a great mystery in this, for the Mother gives birth to the Son of the Father, and the Son recognizes the Holy Bride, who is the image of her Mother. Beholding the Daughter, the Son beholds the Mother; yet Mother Sophia is ever-transcendent and it is the Daughter who is realized.

The Mother remains ever in her purity, without taint, trace, stain, nor mark, and this is also true of the Bride. Yet the Bride becomes everything and everyone, and appears to have taint and trace and stain and mark! The Mother is transparent, but the Daughter is visible light and glory and she is also fire and darkness; though in her inmost essence, the Daughter is the Mother.

Thus it has been said that Logos came for the salvation of Bride Sophia, for it is she who was bound under the dominion of the demiurgos and became the whore to the archons and even to Satan. Is not Logos the presence of awareness through which cosmic ignorance is dispelled and Wisdom nature recognized, thus enlightening and liberating the soul? A great mystery is revealed in this, for in the inmost secret teachings, the Mother and the Son and the Bride are merely personifications—what they are exists within you and is your own bornless nature. This is called the Gnosis of Melchizedek.[13]

St. Mary Magdalene sought to impart these inmost secret teachings after the Lord's ascension. Even among the chosen apostles, few would listen and hear the secret teachings from her because she was a woman. Indeed! Rejected, the Bride was labeled a "whore" in the ignorance of men!

Our Lady and the Angel of Wisdom

Lord Yeshua taught and initiated Lady Mary. But she also received teachings and initiations directly from the Holy Spirit, and also from the spirits of the prophets and angels of God, just as Lord Yeshua received them. More than any of the other prophets, Ezekiel, Isaiah, and Malachi visited her. More than any other archangel, it was Ratziel who ministered to her, for Ratziel is the archangel of Sophia. Indeed, one could well say Ratziel was the holy guardian angel of Our Lady, for she was the incarnation of Christ the Sophia. Thus, all that Ratziel possessed belonged to Our Lady, and whatever she requested from the wisdom treasury, she received. Among the special gifts Ratziel gave to Our Lady was the holy book of his name's sake, the Book of Ratziel, which had once been in the possession of the supernal Adam and Eve. This is a holy book of Pure Kabal,[14] which was reflected on the first holy tablets given to Moses but which was destroyed on account of the golden calf and worship of the demiurge.

To all who received the Bride and who were worthy of such lofty teachings, she taught the mysteries of the Book of Ratziel and she showed them the sacred rites that were in Wisdom's holy book. Nothing was hidden from those who received the teachings and initiations of Sophia's Gospel, for the full power of the company of heaven and all heavenly hosts was bestowed upon them, as upon the Holy Bride.

It was because Lady Mary was in possession of this Book of Ratziel that the Lord knew she could receive all teachings: outer, inner, and secret—for they were, in fact, already known to her. She knew the Ways of Wisdom before he revealed them to her; just as when she spoke a revelation, he also knew it already. Lord Yeshua was the tzaddik[15] of Our Lady, but Ratziel was her maggid.[16] Thus, her education was perfectly complete in the presence of Yahweh and she lacked nothing.

Some masters of the tradition say that what Yeshua added unto Mary was the secret Book of Enoch,[17] of which St. Jude spoke, which is to say, the Gnosis of the Supernal Crown.

Light-Breath of Our Lady

There was light and fire in the breath of Our Lady, the fire of the dragon and the light of the Spirit of Yahweh. With her breath, she devoured unclean and evil spirits and she was able to heal and illuminate those who drew near to her. Merely breathing, she served to enlighten and liberate souls and all were blessed who entered into her presence, whether or not they received her. To the righteous, she was a peaceful angel. To the unrighteous, she was an angel of wrath. To the elect, she was an angel of pure bliss. Such is the very nature of the Shekinah consort of the Lord.

When the Risen Savior breathed the Holy Spirit on the disciples, ordaining them as apostles of Light, he breathed Our Lady upon them. On account of her, they bore the power to bless and to curse, to forgive and to bind, and to work all manner of wonders. This was ordained according to God Most High, all according to the fulfillment of the law and the prophets.

Truly, she is the matrix of Light, as though a prism of light through which the Light-transmission flows, becoming rainbow rays; and all receive the holy stream of the Light-transmission according to their own proper grade. Yet, it is those who receive the Holy Bride in full who are apostles in fullness—for she is the First Apostle and the Apostle of the apostles. She is the Light-transmission of the true apostolic succession.

Now we shall say this of the Holy Bride: She rides in the chariot of Yahweh, which is Elohim, and she rides on the great dragon, which is Leviathan.[18] She is the consort of God and mistress of the dragon. In her holy breath is the power of creation and destruction.

In this we have told a secret, which the wise who invoke our Lady will understand.

Great Beauty

It was quite something that Lady Mary loved the Lord so deeply. She was the most beautiful of women and younger than him, but he was rather plain and almost homely, being weathered by exposure to the elements. No doubt she loved his charm and charisma and could see the great beauty that was in him, of which her own beauty was an outward reflection. She knew he was her one and only love—a True Beloved.

Indeed, uniting herself to him, she became herself and she drew out the greater beauty that was in him, which came from the Supernal crown of Melchizedek. And so it may well be said, they lent one another a spiritual beauty that shone brightly. He was the concealed beauty and she was the revealed beauty, he the spiritual sun and she the kingdom reflecting it. In the mystical embrace of Our Lord and Our Lady, the heavens and earth were united in the Supernal Abode, and the supreme mystery of the bridal chamber was revealed.

May we be blessed to walk in such beauty and holiness as Our Lord and Our Lady!

The Body of Our Lady

The Lord accomplished everything in the body of Our Lady. In her body, he loved and illuminated the world and worked all manner of wonders. When she came to him, she was black. When he poured himself into her, she became white brilliance, for her blackness was pure transparency through which the Light of the Lord shone without obstruction. She is as the window through which the Light of the true cross shines. Joined to him, the image of the Great Seth is revealed— the union of Logos and Sophia. Surely she is Bet El,[19] for the presence of the Lord dwells in her!

It is true. Our Lady had no visible light of her own, for she was Clear Light Joy. Yet in her union with the Lord, she became the glory of rainbow Light. He is the secret center and she is the infinite space in which the Light shines; in their union, she is as the starry night sky—Sophia Stellarum![20]

Our Lady is the holy cup into which Our Lord poured out his blood and living water and into which all true saints also pour out their life's blood. Her body is the Grail of All-Gnosis, and she is the true channel of grace. From her, we drink the Lord and our own true self. We are united with the Lord through her, experiencing movement and repose. This is the basis of the wedding feast (Eucharist) among Sophian Gnostics.

This legend is called "The Veiled Mystery of the Gnostic Mass of Our Lady."

The Maiden of Light

There was a young maiden in the circle of Our Lord and Our Lady whose name was Salome. She was filled with wisdom and knowledge beyond her years, and knew perfectly well who Yeshua and Mary were. Her intelligence was striking, for she could understand all teachings the Lord and Lady spoke, many of which few, if any, disciples understood in full. There was a great light in her, and she was beautiful inwardly and outwardly. She was innocent and pure of heart. Many thought she was an angel accompanying the Lord because she was so near and dear to his heart and was so Beloved by Our Lady. Sometimes, it is said, she was even confused for the Bride, because she so resembled the holiness of Mary and was so close to the Lord.

Lord Yeshua had a very playful spirit, and Salome tended to bring out his playfulness. He could often be like a little child, and they played games together, frequently invoking a contagious laughter because of their humor. When they played, wonders often happened and many among the disciples experienced visions and inspirations. It was quite something to behold!

Lady Mary was the perfect Tzaddik of Salome; for as Thomas was the spiritual twin of the Lord, Salome was the spiritual twin of Lady Mary. Thus, it was Mary who taught and initiated Salome the maiden, and some say she became the successor of Our Lady in the lineage of the Sophian Light-transmission.

Although much delight came to the male disciples on account of Salome's beauty and playfulness, they were never able to understand why Yeshua and Mary spent so much time with her or why they imparted to her inner and secret teachings. They simply could not imagine a soul of such a high grade in a girl. Like the Holy Bride, following the ascension of the Lord, most of the male disciples rejected her testimony of things Lord Yeshua had said to her. Thus, when the Lord departed, Salome became the constant companion of St. Mary Magdalene.

Sophia Nigrans

The masters of the tradition have said that we may contemplate the Song of Solomon as a prophecy of the sacred dance of the Bridegroom and Holy Bride. Therein, we find it written, "I am black and comely, my Beloved . . ." There is a mystery to be spoken concerning this.

Many sought out the Lord but fell away because of the Bride. In truth, the Lord was shameless with her. He caressed her and kissed her in public, and everyone knew she had been a harlot. He put her forth as a priestess-queen, coequal and co-preacher with him. It is said that she is the woman in the Gospels who lets down her hair in public and anoints the body of the Lord in front of one and all in the house! Even many of his close disciples were greatly troubled on account of the Lord's behavior with her, so much so that they would not record her life with him after he departed the world. Yet those who fell away did not understand the nature of Sophia Nigrans.

On the one hand, it is she who leads the soul into the dark nights and mystical death, through which rebirth in the Spirit and unification is attained. On the other hand, because she is the Queen of Demons, she knows how to liberate holy sparks bound in darkness, yet is pure wrath against the evil-doer. In essence, Sophia Nigrans is the contradiction of every preconception, precondition, or expectation of enlightenment. Yet she is the very spirit of enlightenment itself, shattering all illusions of the self-righteous ones. She liberates from every kind of bondage!

It was always the intention of the Lord to outrage, shock, and to challenge religious dogma. Only thus can a spiritual revolution occur and the path to enlightenment actually be revealed. Thus, the Lord took Sophia Nigrans as his Bride, so that all sentimentality and delusions of dogma might be shattered. Although the Lord taught by way of crazy Wisdom, he was ever without sin and walked in perfect beauty and holiness, for in Sophia Nigrans he died and in Sophia Stellarum he was reborn. Such is the true nature of the Bride, Dark and Bright Sophia.

The masters of the tradition have said, "Sophia Nigrans is black to the blind, but white brilliance to the seers." Likewise, they have said that one cannot know the Bright Mother unless one first knows the Dark Mother. This proves a powerful contemplation of the very heart of the Sophian teachings.

Our Lady in Red[21]

It is said that Our Lady wore crimson and scarlet robes with a white inner robe, save during the time of her mourning when her inner robe was black. Golden trim was upon her robes, and she often wore jewels. Fine tattoos were upon her hands and arms, and the sweetest aromas came from her body. Her beauty and glory were enchanting, and her intelligence was thunderous. There were few men who wished to debate with her, for she could swiftly put their intellect to shame.

Although, indeed, she could be wild and was noted as something of a trickster and prankster in her way of imparting the Light-transmission,[22] nevertheless, she was also a woman of great composure, grace, and charm. Truly, she was the image of a great prophetess and priestess-queen, and it was the great presence of fiery light that could make her appear peaceful or blissful or wrathful. She appeared to each person according to the state of that person's own heart and mind.

The power of the Lord was in Mary, for the Lord kept his promise to her and did not change his mind. On the day they first met, he promised, "Into you I will pour out my spirit, and you will bear my gnosis and power in full, and even more than I, you shall have the presence and power of the Queen of Heaven. Thus will the upper and lower Shekinah be joined as one in you and you will be my Bride, Kallah Messiah."

Though, indeed, the living Yeshua is known in full only by way of initiation, some have said that one must also receive initiation to know the Holy Bride. However, they are mistaken. The Holy Bride comes to anyone who calls upon her name, as upon the name of Our Lord, and she appears as the Lady in Red to all who open their minds and hearts to her. She even appears to many, even to little children, who have not invoked her but who in their soul have a secret connection with her. Such is the nature of Our Lady. She gives herself to all who seek to receive her—and so it was when she was with the Lord.

Secret Disciples

The Lord had many secret disciples. Some he taught in their dreams and through vision, others would come to visit him at night, in secret. His inmost disciples he would also teach in secret at night, and St. Mary Magdalene was always with him when he taught in secret, save when she was occupied giving teachings among the women. Thus, she witnessed many wonders others did not, and she heard all teachings the Lord gave among the disciples.

Yeshua had a public face and a private face. Much of what the outer and unspiritual church clings to is only his public face. Following in the way of St. Peter, who rejected the Bride and placed himself as an enemy to her, many secrets and mysteries she had to tell were not received. Of the Lord's secret disciples, such as Joseph of Arimathea, all were faithful and loyal to the Holy Bride and loved her as they loved the Lord, for they knew the Lord often spoke inmost secret things on account of his love for her.

The Second Youth

Two youths captured the heart of the Lord. One was St. Lazarus, who was the wealthy young man the Lord sent on a mystical journey and raised from the dead. The other was a young man the Lord called Malak, meaning "angel." To Lazarus and Malak the Lord taught all manner of mysteries and secret things, and both received initiation from him directly and in private.

This other youth appeared one day and began to follow the Lord at a respectful distance. Wherever the Master went, the boy followed. He watched closely everything the Lord did. Even when the Lord went out in secret to pray, taking only Magdalene with him, the boy would follow so that he might make the prayer of the Lord his own.

At first, the Lord did not speak to him directly, but let the boy follow like his shadow. One evening, however, he asked Mary to use her enchantment power to draw the boy in, and he charged John to go out with Mary and baptize the boy at sunset. He said to them, "When the boy is received, bring him to me." And so Mary and John did as the Lord requested of them.

When they returned with the boy, the Lord took him aside and instructed him in private. He did this for five nights, until the Shabbat eve. Then he sent the boy to Mary and told him to ask her for the final initiation. On the last evening the boy was with Yeshua, he stayed with him all night, and then he stayed with Mary all night, until the morning of the Shabbat. Quite naturally, the young man understood all teachings he received perfectly. Then he went to following the Lord as before, though now with a special light about him. Even on the night of the Passion he followed the Lord, until a temple guard tried to lay hold upon him. Shedding his robe, the boy ran away naked.

The boy never spoke to any disciple except St. Mary Magdalene. It is said that, when the Lord departed the world, the boy then followed her, even into her exile in southern France. According to the masters of the tradition, this young man was among her closest disciples. Some say that he eventually was married to Salome the maiden. (Others say Salome became the wife and consort of St. Michael, and that this young man became the consort of Lady Mary after the ascension of the Lord.)

Seven Faces of the Holy Bride

The Holy Bride has seven faces, the principal face being Our Lady in Red, St. Mary Magdalene. But she also has six other faces, all of which were embodied in Lady Mary—three bright faces and three dark faces. The three bright faces are the Maiden of Light, Mother of the Royal Blood, and Crone of Ancient Knowledge; the three dark faces are the Mistress of the Night, Queen of Demons, and Hag of the Void.

These are as seven veils of Bride Sophia. Unless the Holy Bride reveals herself to a person, those who know her cannot speak the mysteries of her seven faces. It is she who must choose her lovers and bring them into herself.

Without breaking our vows to her, however, we can say this: These faces correspond to the seven rays of the Light-transmission, and within every face there are seven faces; thus there are forty-nine faces of Bride Sophia. The fiftieth face of Sophia is Mother Sophia, and those who behold it attain the perfection of understanding called Primordial Wisdom. Of these it is said, "Their crowns are in their heads."

Let one who seeks to understand this invoke the Holy Bride, seek her revelation, and contemplate deeply what is said here. Remember what the Lord said, "Seek and you will find; ask and you will receive; knock and the door will be open unto you." The Holy Bride is the everlasting door, the gate of all-gnosis.

The Father and the Mother

In public, the Lord spoke of the Father. In private, he spoke of the Mother, for surely it is fitting for the Son to speak openly of his Father but only privately of his Mother. Lady Mary, however, spoke openly of the Divine Mother, as is fitting for a Daughter to do, and she revealed many great mysteries of God the Mother to those who would listen and hear—both the Supernal Mother and our earthly mother.

Our Lady and St. Philip

There were a few male disciples close to Our Lady; St. Philip was among them. One evening, the Lord said to Mary, "It is time to take Philip on his journey." Lady Mary rose and went to Philip and said, "The Lord has given us the word to go upon a journey. Come, let us be going." She led Philip out into the wilderness. It was the new moon and the stars shone brightly in the night sky. She engraved a circle and charged Philip to dig a fire pit and build a fire in it.

When everything was prepared, they sat together in the circle and began to chant the names of God and to pray and meditate together. Philip was drawn into a very deep trance, as though asleep, but was startled from his slumber when Mary leapt up, screeching and screaming and howling and dancing around the fire. Then she began to sing in such a tone and voice as he had never heard. He gazed at her and her whole body became as though formed of flames, the whole circle was on fire, and many wild creatures and beasts gathered around the circle. Even the stars began to dance with her. Beams of light came down from the stars; Mary's body shone with light. It was as though her body was the starry night sky, yet at the same time the body of a star composed of fiery light. A light streamed forth from her heart and penetrated Philip's heart, so that Philip became luminous and filled with light, though not so bright as the body of Our Lady.

Then Philip was taken up in divine rapture and began to dance with Mary. The light continued to pour into him until he shone as bright as the Holy Bride. His body became fiery light, like her divine body, and she merged with him completely, so that her mind became his mind, her heart became his heart, and her body his body. Thus united with her, he was united to Yeshua Messiah. The whole earth and the heavens were in him, as in Our Lady and Our Lord.

When the sun arose in the morning, Philip found himself seated in the circle and Lady Mary seated on the other side, smiling at him. Philip asked her, "Mistress, was that a dream I had of our dance, or did it happen in the world as I saw it?" Mary said, "All things dissolve into their own proper root, from which their essence is drawn, and everything transpires in consciousness, in the soul. Whether in dream or this world or the afterlife, it is the same. Knowing this, you will never taste death. Perhaps, dear brother, you are dreaming this world, and for a little while in the night, you awoke from your dream!"

Then Mary instructed him how to perfect this knowledge and swore him to secrecy. When they returned to the Lord, it was noon, and the Lord and the disciples were eating. Mary and Philip also ate with the Lord, but said nothing of what had transpired that night, though some of the disciples inquired where they had gone.

This was one of five initiations Lady Mary gave to St. Philip. There were a few others the Lord sent out with her: St. Andrew, St. Thomas, St. John, St. Jude, and Malak, the young man Our Lady and Lord loved. Even among the women disciples, few were drawn into this inner and secret continuum of the Light-transmission.

Earthly and Heavenly Powers

As we know, Our Lady was born to a wealthy family, and because of her beauty and intelligence, she attracted the attention of wealthy and powerful men. Thus, she became a very wealthy woman. Her wealth became the power of the Divine Kingdom, for with it she funded the circle of the Master—his heavenly wealth and her earthly wealth being an immense power for the great work. It is a very rare thing that a wealthy person elects to use her or his wealth for the sake of the Divine Kingdom, or even that a wealthy person truly seeks to turn to the Spirit. The love of money and power is an intoxicant. Thus many forget the love of God and one's neighbor on account of it. It is for this reason that the Lord had much to say concerning the wealthy and the businessperson. It is witness to the great soul of Light incarnate in the person of the Bride that she knew her wealth belonged to the One Life-power. How wonderful it is when material powers are used for the sake of the great work, for then they are delivered from the dominion of the demiurgos and archons and restored to the Most High. This is true of any material power that can be named.

Although Our Lady had earthly wealth, she also had heavenly wealth, and because of her heavenly wealth, her earthly wealth was true wealth. This is akin to her beauty. Because of her inward beauty, she was completely beautiful, and because of the Light in her, she drew the Bridegroom to herself! In every way, the inner and outer matched and were in harmony in Our Lady. Thus, it is rightly said that she embodied the Spirit of Truth, for one embodies the Spirit of Truth when one is the same on the inside as on the outside, and the two are established in the Truth and Light.

. Many who are wealthy are not wealthy, many who are beautiful are not beautiful, and so it is with any such quality one can name. Unless the quality is present inwardly, then its outward appearance is a lie and is false. Many in this world who are wealthy and beautiful and powerful will have neither wealth nor beauty nor power in the world to come. Yet, this does not mean that earthly powers are inherently evil or false. Such things are what they are because of the person who possesses them, whether they serve the Truth and Light or give way to falsehood and darkness.

This we learn from Our Lady, in whom all material powers were good and true and righteous, even her sexual desire, which was purely for the Beloved. In this regard, she is the image of true humanity in a woman's form, just as Lord Yeshua is the image of true humanity in a man's form.

The masters of the tradition say that Christhood is simply becoming a true human being, as in the case of Yeshua and Mary. This was constantly at the heart of the teachings of Our Lady and Our Lord.

Perfection of Acquaintance

Those who received teachings and initiation from both Lord Yeshua and Lady Mary entered into perfect acquaintance with the Christ-presence, having acquaintance with Logos and Sophia. However, those who received from Lord Yeshua alone had only partial acquaintance, lacking the knowledge of Sophia. Many came into the acquaintance of Christ the Logos; few became acquainted with Christ the Sophia.

Thus, from the beginning, an outer and unspiritual church arose as a husk to the inner and spiritual church, and an inner and secret order came into being. The outer and unspiritual church has the Word of God, but is lacking in Divine Wisdom. It is the interior church that is in possession of the Wisdom of God, for therein the Bride and Bridegroom are received and through Wisdom comes the perfection of love and power and knowledge—hence the inner and secret order of the mystery.

Knowledge of the Name

The Lord initiated every disciple according to the disciple's capacity. To some, he gave the fullness of the outer; to others he gave something of the inner; and to a few he gave deep things. All knew the name of the Lord and had the power of the name, but only those whom he chose acquired understanding. When he wished a disciple to understand, he would initiate that person, and he would call that person at night to an inner baptism. With chant and prayer and holy meditation, he would uplift the disciple from one joy to another, until the Spirit entered into the disciple and understanding of the blessed name was imparted. To all who received the knowledge and understanding of the name in this way, the Lord would have Lady Mary communicate the inmost secret knowledge of her holy name so that their understanding might be complete. These were the disciples who attained power over the entirety.

Transformation of the World

While the Lord lived, Lady Mary withheld herself, letting glory and honor go fully to the Lord and the Living Father. She worked in secret to accomplish everything behind the scenes. She taught the women disciples how to pray and meditate, and of the holiness of womanhood in the Light-presence. She showed them how to transform every worldly activity into an action of the Spirit and Light, so that, in all that they did, they might cleave to the Lord and worship in Spirit and Truth. Even drawing water from a well or preparing food became an activity of the Kingdom of Heaven among the women disciples, all on account of the teachings of the Holy Bride.

Hidden Matrix

Magdalene was the holy Tzaddik of all the women of the circle. Whenever they had a question on the teachings or sought initiation, they came to her. She taught them mystical prayer and the way of the Divine names and all manner of mysteries. The women with St. Mary Magdalene formed the hidden matrix of light, grounding Supernal Grace in the world and serving as the throne of the Anointed. This became clear in the night of the Passion and on the day of the Pentecost, when the women worked with the Mother and Mary in secret to fulfill the Divine plan and receive the Pleroma of Light in the world.

Peter and the Adversary

It is well known that Peter often acted as the agent of the adversary, for it was to Peter that the Lord said, "Satan, get you behind me!" So it was that Peter often spoke against St. Mary Magdalene among the male disciples, turning many away from her. Often, he questioned the Lord about her and asked the Lord to send her away from the assembly. It was all on account of insecurity and jealousy; for what Peter struggled to comprehend, Mary understood perfectly. He was to St. Mary Magdalene what Judas was to Lord Yeshua; except Judas at one time loved the Lord and Peter always despised Our Lady. It would come to pass that, on account of him, the sacred circle would be divided after the ascension of the Lord.

Our Lady and St. Jude

You will notice that in the Bible of the outer and unspiritual church, with the exception of St. John, little is said of those male disciples who were close to St. Mary Magdalene. Were they to be spoken of, St. Mary Magdalene would also have to be spoken of, because they received the Gospel from her as much as from the Lord.

It is well known that St. Jude received teachings and initiations from the Lord concerning the Secret Book of Enoch. Receiving these secret teachings, he also sought out Mary to learn the secrets of the Book of Ratziel, which was known to her. Thus, St. Jude passed much time in study and practice with Our Lady, perfecting his knowledge, understanding, and wisdom. So it was with several of the male disciples. They sought her out to listen and hear secret teachings she received in private from the Lord.

Earthly and Heavenly Partnership

Because Lady Mary was the constant companion of the Lord, he confided in her and spoke with her about every movement of the Gospel before it transpired. Thus, she always knew what would come to pass before it happened and, with prayer and meditation, supported every action of the Lord, nurturing and guarding every aspect of the Lord's Divine labor. Indeed! She was secretly involved in everything that transpired. She joined her Light to his Light in every wonder-working act and every event. It was a true earthly and heavenly partnership, so that they were one flesh and one soul of Light.

The Perfect Disciple

Although, indeed, Mary was the wife and consort of the Anointed, coequal and co-preacher with him, and embodied Christ the Sophia, nevertheless, Mary was the perfect disciple of the Lord and was humble before the presence of the Lord. Even when the Lord died and was raised up and ascended and she became the true master of the assembly, she spoke of him as her Lord and Master and Savior and did not put herself before him. She exalted Lord Yeshua and humbled herself, knowing the true reception of the Bride would not come to pass until the time of the Second Coming. So it is with every true and faithful disciple, she or he never conceives of her or himself as greater than her or his beloved Tzaddik; and so it was with St. Mary of Magdal. We exalt Our Lady, but she was ever humble and exalted Our Lord.

Notes

1. Literally, "Divine fullness."

2. Literally, "good luck," a Jewish wedding custom.

3. Klippot, in Hebrew, indicates the dominion of impure emanations and the dark and hostile forces.

4. Literally, "Lord," a Hebrew divine name used in place of Yahweh.

5. Twin indicating an inmost male disciple, as open and receptive to the teachings of the Master as Magdalene.

6. Mysteries of sexual mysticism and magic in the Kabbalah.

7. Gnostic adept.

8. Gnostic master.

9. Rapturous spiritual union or spiritual cleaving.

10. Literally, "anointed bride."

11. Literally, "healing" or "mending."

12. The circle of disciples of Yeshua and Mary.

13. The body of inmost secret teachings of enlightenment among Sophians.

14. Literally "revelation" or "tradition."

15. Spiritual master.

16. Angelic teacher.

17. Specifically, the Hebrew Book of Enoch, which is said to have been an oral tradition at the time.

18. Literally, "destroyer."

19. Literally, "the house of God."

20. Literally, "starry wisdom."

21. A gnostic title for the Holy Bride.

22. A term in Gnosticism for teachings and initiations, as well as the transmission of living presence and power.

CYCLE 4

THE HOLY BRIDE AND
THE MYSTERIES

The Divine Incarnation

Lord Yeshua and Lady Mary share the same birth, for they were both born of the womb of Mother Sophia. So it is with all who are anointed with the Supernal Light; they are born of the womb of Primordial Wisdom and are called children of Light. Thus, Yeshua and Mary share the same Mother and they share the same Father, the Living Father which is the infinite and eternal.

They are one soul of Light and one person of Light, though appearing as male and female. They come from the Light-continuum, entering into the world as Light-bearers, so that we might also know ourselves as souls of Light and persons of Light and remember our origin in the Supernal Abode. Yeshua and Mary are a man and a woman, fully human. Yet embodying the Light-presence, they are pure and holy emanations of Light and are more than human. So it is with everyone who is anointed with the Supernal Light and who embodies the Light-presence, they also become pure and holy emanations of the Light-continuum.

We may speak of the birth of Our Lord and Our Lady, and we may speak of their life stories, just as we may speak of our own birth and life story. Yet all of this transpires in a world of shadows and shades, the Truth and Light being within, yet ever beyond the appearance of this world. Indeed, this world is a play of light and shadow under the dominion of the demiurgos and archons, but the World of Supernal Light is within and beyond this world. The light and shadows in this world are but a dim reflection of the transparent Light of the Supernal World.

In truth, Our Lord and Our Lady are without father or mother, and they have no past. They are pure and bornless beings. They are the Light-presence at repose in the Light-continuum and the Light-presence in movement within the realm of ever-becoming; and thus so also are we who receive the Word and Wisdom of the infinite and eternal—we who look within to recognize and realize the Light-presence in us.

From the time of the First Coming to the time of the Second Coming, the Divine Incarnation continues to transpire. This Divine Being called Christos or Light-presence continues to be realized and embodied in human beings. Those who embody it are united with Our Lord and Our Lady, as though one body and one soul—hence the mystical body of the Anointed.

In the name of the Lord, St. Mary Magdalene said, "Our Living Father is Light and our Divine Mother is the Pleroma of Light, and the Aeons of Light[1] are our brothers and sisters; and so it is with all the children of Light." When the Lord was speaking to Nichodemus about those reborn of the Mother Spirit and Nichodemus could not comprehend the teachings of the Lord, the Lord said to him, "Very truly I tell you, we speak of what we know and testify to what we have seen; yet you do not receive our testimony. If I have told you about earthly things and you do not believe, how can you believe if I tell you about heavenly things?"[2]

Now here, we are speaking of the true mystery behind the appearance of Our Lord and Our Lady, and of the very heart of the Gospel of Truth, and we are speaking of the mystery behind our own appearance in the world. For this reason, Lady Mary would often say, "Look within and beyond the Lord to see the true image of Christ, and look within and beyond you to see the Truth and Light in yourself."

The Light and the Darkness

Yeshua was born into the light and Mary was born into the darkness. Thus, when Our Lord and Our Lady met and entered into union, light and darkness were transcended and the True Light was revealed. Yeshua was male and Mary was female. Thus, when they united, male and female were transcended and the true image of the Human One was revealed, which is the true image of Light.

The duality of light and darkness, male and female, and all apparent opposites is the foundation of the dominion of the demiurgos and archons. Joining together all opposites in their mystical embrace, Our Lord and Our Lady put an end to the dominion of the demiurgos and archons, transcending it. This is the mystery of the love-play of Our Lord and Our Lady.

Some have said the Lord is the Soul of Light and Mary is the material body, which, when joined to the Soul of Light, becomes a Body of Light. This is a worthy contemplation, for the mystery of the body of the resurrection and the secret of the great ascension is contained within it.

The Beginning of the Gospel

Some have said that the birth of the Lord is the beginning of the Gospel. Others say that the beginning of the Gospel is the baptism of the Lord, which is the call for the Bride to return from her exile. Some assert that the Gospel begins with the first wonder-working act of the Lord, which was the entrance of the Bride into the holy land. Still others say that the Gospel begins when Our Lord and Our Lady meet and unite, because the Gospel flows forth from the love-play of the Bridegroom and Bride.

The masters of the tradition say that there is truth in all of these views, yet that, truly, the Gospel begins when we receive it and the Truth and Light is manifest in our own experience.

Baptism and Temptation

The baptism of Mary happened when she was in Babylon, for the baptism is the inner experience of Light descending from above. It was for this reason that the angel of John the Baptist went to Mary to call her in from her exile. When the Light descended upon Lord Yeshua in his baptism at the Jordan River, in the Spirit, John saw the Light descend on Mary also. Therefore, the prophet John recognized that Yeshua was the Messiah and that Mary was Kallah Messiah, the Anointed Bride.

When the Light descends upon a person, the darkness in a person rises up to oppose the Light, and a struggle ensues as the person seeks to enter fully into the Light-presence. Thus, when Yeshua was in the wilderness being tempted by Satan, Mary was also in the wilderness wrestling with the adversary.

This is true throughout the Gospel, for Yeshua and Mary shared the experience of every event in the Gospel and of every cycle of the eightfold initiation[3] into Supernal or Messianic consciousness. Indeed, they were completely interdependent and interconnected and served to open the way to one another, each an integral part of the divine revelation. We cannot speak of one without also speaking of the other. They are one holy soul and one Light-presence.

Vision of the Sermon on the Mount

Lord Yeshua ascended the holy mount with Lady Mary. When they sat down, the disciples ascended to join them, both men and women disciples. The winds ceased, all clouds vanished from the sky, and the sun and moon shone brightly in the day. An electrical energy filled the air and peace entered into all who were present, a perfect clarity and peace in the heart and mind. Yeshua was like unto the Light, Mary was like unto a prism of Light, and all of the disciples were like rays of Light, both the men and women alike. It was an image of Rainbow Glory.

The image of the great angel Hua[4] appeared in the sky, and Raphael stood in the east, Gabriel in the west, Michael in the south and Uriel in the north. A great luminous assembly of heavenly hosts filled endless space in all directions. Adam and Eve, the spirits of the patriarchs and matriarchs, and the spirits of all the prophets were present in the subtle dimension and all souls from future generations who would enter into the Light-continuum. A great Light-presence was within and all around Our Lord and Our Lady, and the Light pervaded the good earth, so that, as long as the Lord was giving the sermon, there was peace and joy throughout the world.

As Yeshua Messiah spoke, the hosts of earth and heaven worshipped in the presence of Yahweh, and the heavens and earth were united in mystical embrace. The Spirit of Yahweh was in Lord Yeshua and Lady Mary, for, united, they were the image of Adonai. The celestial dew of white brilliance poured down through the image of the great angel of the Lord and rained down upon all who were gathered. The fragrance of roses and heavenly flowers filled the air. It was as though the supernal image of Miriam's well appeared upon the holy mount and living water flowed out of it, giving life and light to the people and the land. Indeed! It was the image of the Second Coming within the First Coming, the fulfillment of the law and the prophets. All of this was within and behind the words Lord Yeshua spoke on that holy day. The wise will understand the meaning of this, and the Holy Spirit will reveal the mystery to all who seek it.

It is said that, with ten holy utterances, God created the heavens and the earth and the human one. At the Sermon on the Mount, with ten holy utterances, the Anointed generated a new heaven and new earth and new human being, for the supernal perfection of the Second Adam was revealed. With Ten Commandments, the faithful were bound to the law, but with Ten Blessings, the Anointed set the elect free from bondage to the dominion of the demiurge and archons. Until the Living Word entered into the world and Daughter Sophia was uplifted and redeemed, the prophets could not receive the divine revelation in its purity. Always, the vision and voice were tainted and corrupted by the influence of the demiurge and archons. How else could the God of love, mercy, and compassion command war and vengeance or incite people to genocide and all manner of slaughtering of human beings and beasts without just cause? For this reason, the Word and Wisdom of God became incarnate, to deliver souls from bondage to the dominion of falsehood and ignorance. Thus, the Lord spoke the sermon of Light for all to hear and showed forth the true image of the Light for all to see who had eyes to see. Truly, the Transfiguration happened during the Sermon on the Mount, but there were none who had eyes to look and see it.

The world worships the dominion of the demiurgos and archons, but the elect worship the Alien God, El Elyon. The dominion of the demiurgos and archons was shattered on the day the sermon of Light was spoken; for those who listen and hear it are no longer the slaves to cosmic ignorance.

All of this the Lord spoke for Mary's sake and all of this the Lord spoke in Wisdom.

Six Holy Women

Three women called Mary were the constant companions of the Lord: Mary the Mother, Mary the Old Woman, and St. Mary Magdalene. Three others were also with him much of the time and their name was Salome: Salome the Maiden, Salome the Wise, and Salome the Elder. Mary is a name connected to Marrah, the Bitter Sea, and Salome is connected to Shalom, Peace. Mem, which is the principal letter in Mary, is water. Shin, which is the principal letter in Salome, is fire. And we know that the Lord baptized with water and with fire and with the Spirit.

Thus, Yeshua walked always with the Depth of Wisdom and Depth of Peace, and these six holy women were present with him when he was teaching and initiating—the Matrix of the Living Word.

Now we may say that there were six emanations of Sophia through which the Living Word flowed: the Primordial Sophia, Great Mother Sophia, Mystery Sophia, Knowledge Sophia, Faith Sophia, and Love Sophia. All of these had their male counterpart in the Lord, Christ the Logos, and they were the Matrix of Space in which the Gospel transpired.

Mother Mary was the space of all Sophia and all who were called "Mary" were in her, Mary Magdalene was the display of all Sophia, and all who were called Salome were in her. Sophia emanates from Sophia, as the Daughter from the Mother; Logos is born of Sophia and is fulfilled by Sophia, and it is Sophia that Logos imparts.

Logos is the image of the Father; Sophia is the image of the Mother. In the Holy One of Being, there is no difference between Logos and Sophia, for they are one in the Supernal Crown.

Three Holy Mountains

The Sermon, the Transfiguration, and the Crucifixion all take place on the holy Mountain of Initiation, and the wisdom of the three holy women called "Mary" corresponds to the threefold Mountain of Initiation. The Mount of the Sermon is Mary Magdalene, the Mount of the Transfiguration is Mother Mary, the Mount of the Crucifixion is Mary the Old Woman, and all of these are the holy womb. It has been said, "The womb and the tomb are one." Thus, the empty tomb, which is the womb giving birth to the Risen Savior, is the union of all three Wisdoms.

St. Mary Magdalene is the first to glimpse the Risen Savior because the true sermon of the Gospel is spoken by him on the holy Mount of the Ascension, and she is the Wisdom of the Gnostic preacher.

The Magical Display

Yeshua showed many great wonders. He drove darkness out of the people and the land, healed all manner of disease, and extended the Fire and Light of the Supernal Abode, illuminating the world. He commanded the elements, walked on water, transformed water into wine, and fed thousands with a few loaves and fishes. All of these things he did to show the true nature of reality, which is fluid and ever changing and which is all a play of light and shadow, and all of it was the manifestation of his Shekinah consort, the Holy Bride—St. Mary Magdalene. Was it not all the magical display of Wisdom, and is this not the true nature of creation? For it is written, "The Lord founded everything on Wisdom."

The Transfiguration

The purpose of the Gospel was the Transfiguration and Resurrection, which is the revelation of the truth of the Supernal Soul of Light. It was for the sake of this Light-transmission that the Living Word and Wisdom of God entered into the world. Everything the Lord did was for the sake of this. All along, his aim was to prepare the disciples to receive the Light-transmission, and Lady Mary was his partner in this great work.

When it was time, the Lord took a few of his close male disciples along with St. Mary Magdalene up on top of a holy mountain. He was transfigured before them into a Light-image, showing his close companions the Pleroma of Light and the Light-continuum. The men were afraid and wished to shelter themselves from the glory and power. Thus Peter asked if they could build tabernacles for the radiant Christos and the Light-images that appeared with him. Then the men fell unconscious, overwhelmed by the glory of the Truth and Light, but St. Mary Magdalene was not overwhelmed and remained awake in the Light-presence.

What the men beheld was merely the outset of the divine revelation. Because they fell unconscious, they did not receive the Light-transmission, and the Light-transmission passed to Lady Mary. She beheld the whole divine revelation, and she herself shone with visible glory. In their brief glimpse, the men thought Elijah and Moses appeared. In truth, it was Elijah and Enoch, the two masters of the ascension. Mary bore witness of the Light-images, though later the men would not believe her testimony.

First, the Lord showed Mary the Light-images in the World of Supernal Light, and then the heavens and earth in his Body of Light. Then he took her soul up in himself and revealed the Aeons of Light and Pleroma of Light, and the beginning and end of all creation, and the truth of the One-Without-End, the glory and splendor of which is the Light-continuum. She beheld the World of Supernal Light above, below, and everywhere in between, and knew it all within her own body as in the image of the Lord. Thus, the Transfiguration became the consummation of their mystical union, and they became fully one Light-presence in the world on that holy day.

Because Mary was with the Lord all of the time, shared the most intimate moments with him, and saw many secret wonders, she had beheld him shining with Supernal Light and show forth great mysteries many times before, things the men could not endure until the cross. Yet, it was on the holy mountain that he revealed everything, all at one time, and fulfilled his promise to pour himself into her. It was this that made many of the male disciples most jealous of all, for she walked with the full presence and authority of the Anointed from that day on.

The Lord swore the disciples who were with him at the Transfiguration to secrecy, though they were clearly shaken by what they witnessed. They came down the mountain dazed and silent, but the Holy Bride descended in holy awe and wonder; his love fulfilled such as no mortal man could fulfill it. She would later speak of this to her disciples, saying, "This is the love men and women seek to fulfill through mortal relationships, which is only fulfilled in the intimate embrace of the Spiritual Sun. This is the true yearning in the depth of every soul, and yet men and women fear it."

Transfiguration of the Bride

Mary was also transfigured on the mount with the Lord. Yet like the Lord, she concealed the fullness of the Light-presence as she walked in the world, save when a soul was ready for harvest and desired to receive the living presence and power in full. Then, like the Lord, she would reveal the Truth and Light and impart the Light-transmission. One is Christian until one receives the Light-transmission from an apostle of Light, but one becomes Christed when the Light-transmission is received. When one embodies the Light-presence in full, one becomes Christ.

On the evening of the Transfiguration, Mary chose three inmost women disciples and took them to a sacred cave. Salome the maiden was among them, and some say Martha. When they entered into the cave, Lady Mary began speaking the mysteries of the Christos and the Supernal Abode. She was transfigured before them and shone with visible light and glory as the Lord did upon the holy mountain.

The Light-images of Lilith and Eve appeared, and Sarah and the prophetess Miriam, and the great image of Grandmother Israel. A crown of twelve stars was on Our Lady's head, she stood upon the crescent moon, and she revealed the World of Supernal Light and all that was to come to pass, even the mysteries of the Second Coming and New Jerusalem. The women remained conscious and awake, abiding in holy awe and wonder. When the revelation was complete, the women worshipped in the presence of Yahweh, and the eldest woman said, "Truly, you are the glory of the Great Mother and the redemption of all womanhood; you are the Mother of Life, Holy Wisdom. Blessed are you and blessed is the Lord, the Great Seth![5] Praise God Most High!"

When the women who were with Mary came out of the cave in the morning, their faces shone with visible light, so that for several days they had to conceal themselves. Mary returned to the Lord's side. Embracing her, he said to her, "It is very good. Now all things must be fulfilled." When he spoke these words, she knew what he meant. Soon after, he concluded his public ministry after raising Lazarus from the dead and tended only to those given to him by the Holy Spirit.

The Anointing of the Lord's Body

There is much confusion in the holy books of the outer and unspiritual church concerning the woman who anointed the Lord's body with costly perfume, but among Gnostics of the inner and secret order, there is no confusion at all. It was St. Mary of Magdal, his wife and consort. The telltale sign is that she let her hair down, which would only be proper for a wife and consort to do, though, even for a wife, it was a questionable act in those days if done in front of others.

A great mystery lies behind this action. It was an act of love and devotion, yet it was a magical act at the same time. In so doing, Mary made the Lord's body the talisman of a holy sacrifice for the sake of the elect and the Soul of the World.

Born into a profane family, binding herself to the cross of the world and descending into the heart of darkness, Lady Mary linked the world and darkness to herself, so that, being uplifted, the Soul of the World and holy sparks bound in husks of darkness might also be uplifted. Though she was not killed in body, she was slain in her soul. Thus in her soul, she had died and been resurrected. So it is said that she opened the way for the death and resurrection of the Lord. When she anointed the Lord's body, she linked his body to the Soul of the World and to all of the darkness that is in it, so that, crucified, all of the darkness should also be crucified and the spell of death put to an end, and so that the Soul of the World might be uplifted from the dominion of the demiurgos in the resurrection and ascension.

Thus, she acted as a priestess-queen preparing the body of a holy priest-king for sacrifice, his blood and flesh given over to the demiurgos and archons as ransom for those souls he sought to liberate from their dominion, and for the sake of binding the serpent in cessation. Thus, with him, she was making a holy sanctuary for the souls of the elect throughout time who might cleave to the Anointed and also become the Anointed.

This is a great mystery that only Sophia can reveal to a person, for through the cross, the Lord severed the cords that bound his disciples away from receiving the Light-transmission. More than a holy sacrifice for the dissolution of sin, it was the action of the divine revelation. Only in this way would all the disciples receive the Light-transmission in full and understand its true meaning. What could not be fulfilled by the Transfiguration was to be fulfilled by the Resurrection.

There was great spiritual power in the act of Our Lady anointing the body of Our Lord, yet also it was her offering him up and letting go of her Beloved—her own sacrifice, such as only a woman and wife would comprehend. The men who witnessed the magical act of Our Lady did not know what she was doing, but the Holy Mother who saw it understood, as did Salome the maiden and Martha.

The Conception of St. Michael

It is generally held that Our Lady and Our Lord conceived St. Michael, their son and the heir of the lineage of royal blood, on the eve of the Shabbat the week before the drama of the Passion and Crucifixion. Thus, at the Crucifixion and Resurrection, and while the Risen Savior appeared until the time of the final Ascension, Lady Mary was with child, having St. Michael in her womb. The Holy Bride had become the Holy Mother—the mother of a supernal humanity.

The School of St. Lazarus, however, holds a different view. According to St. Lazarus, St. Michael was conceived by the Risen Savior from a seed of light emanated into the womb of the Holy Bride. According to this Gnostic school of thought, St. Michael emanated from the heart-womb of Our Lady the instant he was conceived, not as a child of the earth, but a child of the Supernal Abode—hence the name Michael, which means "Who-Is-Like-Unto-God."

Some have said that the Lady Mary conceived and gave birth to twins, a son and a daughter, and that the son emanated from her heart-womb and her daughter was born of her actual womb, the two resembling one another perfectly. Others have said that St. Michael was a hermaphrodite, being both male and female in one body, the actualization of the androgynous one, the Second Adam.

In any case, it is generally held that Yeshua and Mary bore children of their union, and that these children formed a lineage of royal blood, the holy blood of Christ being transmitted directly into the human life-wave, as well as mystically and magically through the rite of the wedding feast.[6] This is one of the esoteric meanings of St. Mary Magdalene as the Holy Grail.

All of these views speak of the Mystery of St. Michael and the nature of initiations in the Gnostic Order of St. Michael.

Perfection of Pregnancy

It has often been said that, when a woman is pregnant, she is radiant and most beautiful, perhaps in the perfection of her beauty and power. This was especially true of St. Mary Magdalene, who, in the conception of her child, knew the Lord most intimately, for when she conceived, having the most intimate knowledge of the Lord, she became completely perfect. As St. Michael grew in her womb, she ascended from one state of perfection to another and from one glory of beauty to another, so that, giving birth to One-Who-Is-Like-Unto-God, she was the perfection of perfection, which is to say the Perfect Aeon[7] of the world-to-come.

This is the perfection of all who know the Living Yeshua most intimately, who rise from grade to grade, from light to light, into the Perfect Aeon of Light, and then bring the Supernal Light down and give birth to it in the world. It is said that all of the elect are born of the intimate knowledge between the Lord and Anointed Bride.

Yet, there is another mystery, more esoteric; for if Our Lady was transfigured and was a Woman of Supernal Light, what would be the nature of the child born of her womb? If Mother Mary gave birth to Yeshua but was not yet a Woman of Light, then what sort of man would St. Michael be, or would any child of Our Lady become? Some have said that the prophet among the apostles, St. John, beheld this mystery and wrote it in the Book of the Apocalypse. It is St. Mary Magdalene who is the Woman of Light, the Mother of the Elect, who is called the Mother of the Royal Blood. Of this secret mystery, we cannot openly speak. It can only be spoken to those who know it already and only if they are wise with the Gnosis of Bride Sophia.

The Dreadful Task of Judas

Many say that Judas betrayed the Lord, and this may be true. Yet, having seen the living presence and power of the Lord, why would anyone close to him turn against him? Some have said that it was hostility toward the Holy Bride, kindled by Peter's venomous words, which caused him to betray the Lord. Others say that he did not betray the Lord at all, but that he followed the instructions of the Lord as a true and faithful disciple.

Indeed, it has been said that the Lord called Judas in secret one night, before the events that would transpire, and told Judas what must be done. He chose Judas because he was strong in his faith and close to the Lord and the Bride. Mary was witness to this, but later, when she testified to it before the male disciples, they would not believe her. After all, whatever the cause, the actions of Judas are perplexing, and it is easier to believe in evil than in good.

The Last Supper

Mother Mary and Mary Magdalene, along with the women disciples, prepared the upper room for the Last Supper. They arranged the room, prepared and blessed the bread and wine, lit lamps and burned incense, and consecrated the space as sacred and holy through their love and devotion. Lady Mary Magdalene led them in prayer and meditation. So the Spirit of Holiness came into the room and the

Holy Shekinah dwelt in that place. When the Lord entered, there was light upon light; the sacred space shone with glory. The men and women alike partook of the Last Supper, and all were blessed by the Lord, the high priest of the order of Melchizedek who brought out the bread and wine of his body and blood.

Bread and Wine

The Holy Eucharist is called the wedding feast, because in it we celebrate our gnosis and union with the Living Yeshua. Yet, our mystical union transpires through the Holy Bride, St. Mary Magdalene; thus it is a celebration of the union of the Bridegroom and Bride, which is the true meaning of the symbol of the cross among Sophians.

Some say that the bread is the Lord and the wine is the Bride, on account of the invocation of the Holy Bride when the Lord transformed water into wine. Others say the bread is the Bride and the wine is the Lord, because the bread represents the presence and the wine the essence, and she is the living presence and he the secret essence. In any case, among Sophian Gnostics, the Holy Eucharist is a rite of the order of Melchizedek, and the bread and wine are symbols of Our Lord and Our Lady and the Supernal Grace that flows through them.

Night of Passion

There was great light and great darkness on the Night of Passion, the light of the blessing of Melchizedek and the darkness of the vision of sorrow and suffering of a world about to put the great Light-bearer to death. This was the experience of the men and women disciples on the night of Passion.

Those who cling to the suffering of the Lord and speak often of it may not be lacking in wisdom, for by way of suffering he taught the perfection of Love Wisdom, so that we might know how to love and how deeply the love of the Lord ran. Yet, it may be that there was no suffering. If the Lord was a pure Light-emanation, then only an appearance of an image was upon the cross and the Lord suffered nothing that is conceived of as his suffering. In any case, what the Lord did suffer was the rejection of the True Light by those who love and cleave to the darkness—and so the Lord suffers to this day, along with the Holy Bride in her rejection and exile.

On that night, when the men went out with the Lord to the Garden of Gethsemane, the women disciples remained in the upper room, keeping a vigil of prayer. St. Mary Magdalene led the women in prayer and meditation; they ran and returned, ascending and descending from the heights of joy to the depths of sorrow until the break of day. Of the male disciples, only St. John returned after the Lord's arrest to keep vigil with the Mother, the Bride, and the women disciples, all of the men scattering in fear of their own death. Truly, within and behind the Gospel, the women were the foundation and enduring strength of the sacred circle. Always, they labored in prayer, meditation, and sacred ritual in support of the great work of the Anointed.

Many wondered why the Lord taught and initiated women alongside men. It was because he knew and honored the truth of womanhood and the great power that is in it. Because he loved and honored women, it is no wonder they were so close and faithful to him, even on the night of Passion.

At dawn, Mother Mary, Mary Magdalene, Martha, and John went out to keep vigil with the Lord at Golgotha, though some say it was Salome the maiden and not Martha who went out.

On the Way to Golgotha

Mother Mary, Magdalene, Martha, and John walked to Golgotha slowly, inwardly chanting the names of God and in prayer and meditation, though outwardly in silence. Joy had completely departed. They were in mourning, not for the Lord who had yet to die, but for the people, the land, and the whole world, bound to the dominion of the demiurgos and archons and to perpetual sorrow and suffering. It was not Satan that inspired those who killed the Lord; it was the archons. Yet they did not know what they were doing. Thus, the four mourned the plight of ignorance.

It would be impossible to speak the complexity of feelings and emotions in these holy persons on that day or during the three days that would follow—for there was layer upon layer of feelings, from human to heavenly knowing. So it was among all the disciples of the Lord in that darkest of times in their journey with the Anointed.

The Crucifixion

There are many tales of the crucifixion and many gradations of the Mystery. Yet in all of the tales, St. John is present, along with the Mother, Mary Magdalene, and a third woman. Thus, at the crossing, there is the Maiden, the Mother, and the Crone, the three faces of Great Mother Sophia. Though many would speak of the Living Father raising up the Son from death, according to the masters of the tradition, it was Mother Sophia or, as some say, God the Mother. That St. John was with these three holy women reveals that he was a devotee of the Divine Mother and Mother Spirit, and so when Yeshua was upon the cross, he said to the Mother, "Mother, behold your Son," and he said to St. John, "Son, behold your Mother."

Now others speak another mystery concerning these words. Some say it was the Christos speaking to the Holy Mother and the Christ-bearer, so as to say the Christos was not crucified; rather, it was the Christ-bearer who suffered the Crucifixion. Thus, the Mother of Christ is not Mary but is Mother Sophia or God the Mother. And so it is with all who are Christed, their Mother is Sophia and their Bride is Sophia, and all wisdom of the Ancient Mother is in them.

To have the mother of a son behold the crucifixion of her son or the wife and consort of a man behold the crucifixion of her husband and lover is surely the anguish of a crucifixion of the heart and soul. Thus also did the Mother and Bride experience the grief and pain of crucifixion on that day, and that grief and pain did not cease when the Lord breathed his last. It continued until the day of the resurrection, when their sorrow was transformed into joy and their hope affirmed.

The Holy Grail

St. Mary Magdalene brought the cup from the Last Supper with her to Golgotha. When the Roman centurion pierced the side of the Lord and blood and water poured out of the Lord's side, Lady Mary put the cup to the wound and gathered some of the blood and water into it. When she did this, she was inwardly chanting certain divine names and prayed for the healing of the world, and thus she made and consecrated the Holy Grail.

The Grail remained in the custody of Lady Mary until her death. She used to teach the mysteries and sacred ceremonies of the Grail to her disciples. It healed every form of disease or wound, including the deeper wounds of the soul and spirit, and it granted long life to those who drank from it, among other blessings and boons. Some would say this Holy Grail exists even to this day, and those who say this often claim it is in the treasury of a secret society.

Though many believe in an actual and physical cup, many among Sophians would say that St. Mary Magdalene is the true Holy Grail, for it is into her that Lord Yeshua poured out the divine fullness of the Christ Spirit. Likewise, the Grail is often said to be the sanctuary of the heart of those who receive the Light-transmission and embody the Christ-presence. There seems to be some truth in all of these views.

Holy Relics

There are said to be two principal holy relics from the crucifixion—the Grail that gathered the blood and water flowing from the body of the Lord, and the lance that made the blood and water flow. Mary is said to have held the Grail in sacred trust, and it is said that Joseph of Arimathea obtained possession of the sacred lance. The powers of the lance are never openly spoken, let alone the power of the Grail and lance joined together—but it is said both holy relics continue to exist somewhere.

Lilith at the Crucifixion

It has been said that, when Our Lady anointed the body of the Lord, preparing him as a holy priest-king for his final journey, Lilith leapt out of her and into the Lord. When the Lord was upon the cross, Lilatu leapt out of him and she danced around the Lord upon the cross. Then, she made the top of his skull into a cauldron. Putting his body in it, she made heavenly ambrosia, which she served up to the hosts of heaven.

Then, once again, the Lord appeared on the cross. Lilith leapt out and danced, as before, and again made his skull into a cauldron. However, this time she brewed a strange concoction out of his body, mixing in bitter herbs and all manner of strange things. Then, she let out a yell and called all of the archons and unclean spirits to drink, and so they did.

One final time, the Lord appeared on the cross. Lilatu leapt out screeching and screaming and dancing wildly about, tore his body from the cross, ripped it into pieces, and threw them straight into the mouths of evil creatures and demons.

Thus, Lilith made an offering of the body and blood of the Lord three times, feeding all spirits and appeasing all spirits. Then the Lord appeared above the cross as a great Light-presence in the Jeweled Wisdom Body of Rainbow Glory. The Light poured out upon all living spirits and souls and upon the whole world, and all were satisfied and all were blessed. Thus, the Lord could pass through all domains above, below, and in between, gathering the sparks into his Mystical Body.

In this way, masters of the tradition have indicated the Mystery of the Crucifixion, and they have generated a special practice for the adepti[8] who seek gnosis of this Mystery. Thus, many teachings and practices have been generated from this legend among Gnostic Christians of the Sophian Tradition. It is said to have been a legend begun by St. Mary of Magdal.

The First Stigmatic

When the Lord was upon the cross, the stigmata appeared on the body of Our Lady. She suffered and bled as the Lord suffered and bled, and she wept for the world. Her robes became crimson with the blood of Christ, the Logos and Sophia, so that she was baptized in the holy blood of the Savior. It was a passion of love, even unto death and in death itself, for Our Lady also died upon the cross that day.

It was as though the whole world was passing away: visions of the End-of-Days arose, and all manner of dark and hostile forces assailed her, as though all of the sins and darkness of humankind fell upon her, as upon the body of the Lord. The heart of Our Lady was truly broken. In her heart and soul she knew the supreme mystery being revealed; nevertheless, as a woman she grieved deeply and as the Savioress she grieved yet deeper for the world and the plight of God's creatures under the dominion of cosmic ignorance.

As the Spirit of the Lord passed through the gates of Hades and descended through the realms of Gehenna, so also did the soul of Our Lady. Yet in the world, she kept vigil at the tomb, waiting to gather in the sparks, all the while experiencing the stigmata in full. Thus, St. Mary Magdalene was the first stigmatic, just as she would become the first holy apostle of the Risen Savior.

We may speak of the suffering of Our Lord. Yet with her exile into the pit of darkness in Babylon, her experience of the stigmata, and her later rejection and exile to a foreign land, surely we must also speak of the suffering of Our Lady, which is reflected in the continued plight of womanhood in the world. Likewise, as much as the suffering of the Lord, we must also speak of the suffering of Our Earthly Mother and her good creatures, who continue to suffer the Crucifixion on account of ignorance.

The First Apostle of Light

Lady Mary kept vigil at the tomb of the Lord, arriving just before the break of day and departing just as the sun set each day. On one hand, she was in mourning, wearing an inner robe of black; on the other hand, she was waiting expectantly, for she knew the Lord would rise from among the dead. So it came to pass that it happened just as she expected it to!

On the third day, she arrived just as the sun was ascending over the eastern horizon and she found the stone before the tomb rolled away and the tomb empty. Only the death shroud remained, but the body of the Lord was gone. She went to bear witness to the other disciples, running all the way. The men did not believe her, so they went out to see for themselves, Peter and another disciple out-running all of them. They also found the tomb empty and realized Mary had spoken the truth. They went back to the other disciples and confirmed the tomb was, in fact, empty.

Mary returned to the tomb alone. When she looked into the tomb, she saw two great angels sitting where the Lord's head and feet would be. She instantly recognized the angels to be the archangels of the Crown and Kingdom, though some have said that they were two other archangels. They said to Mary, "Look! The Beloved lives and you are, in truth, the Anointed Bride!" Just then she turned around. The Risen Savior was standing in front of her, and she recognized him instantly, for she had seen him in the body of glory and had beheld the great angel of the Lord.

In that instant, the soul of Lady Mary leapt out of her body, and the Risen Savior carried her with him in ascent, so that she should be perfect in the gnosis of the Risen Christ. Passing up through the domains of the archons, they were invisible. Passing through the seven heavens and the outer and inner chambers of the Palace of Lights, all the heavenly hosts bowed down in worship of the Living Father, the Spiritual Sun, and the Mother Spirit. The soul of Mary entered into the Supernal Abode. The Lord took his Bride into the bridal chamber, and she witnessed the repose of the Son in the Living Father. The Lord said to her, "Join with me, Beloved Bride, and abide in my Father's repose." But she said to the Lord, "I cannot, my Adonai, for many are the living spirits and souls that remain in bondage, and rare, as yet, is the Light fully embodied in womanhood. I am my Mother's Daughter, and I must return. Let it be that I may continue to incarnate in a woman's form until the time of the Second Coming, that, while you abide in repose, I might be set in motion." Thus Our Lady spoke a vow in the Supernal Abode.

Then the Living Yeshua said to his Beloved Bride, "What you have spoken is the will of our Father, and surely it is the grace of our Mother in you. Let it come to pass as you have spoken it. You are truly Kallah

Messiah, and the Light-transmission of the Second Coming shall be made perfect in you, all as you desire." Then he said to her, "Come, my holy bride, let us be going." He led her in descent, restoring her soul to her body. Then the Risen Savior said to Lady Mary, "Go, and tell our brothers and sisters I am coming to them shortly, and let them make ready to receive me." Then Mary went and reported to the disciples all that she had seen and all that the Lord had said, though she did not speak of her vow or her more intimate conversation with the Lord. Although she spoke the truth to them, the men did not believe her until the Risen Savior appeared to them directly. Though the Lord chastised them for their unbelief, nevertheless, after the Lord's ascension, most of the men would later reject the Holy Bride.

Thus, the Risen Savior ordained St. Mary Magdalene as the first apostle, and as the apostle of the apostles. On account of her vow, it is said that she continues to incarnate in a woman's form in every generation. The masters of the tradition say that she is here with us now, in this present generation.

The Appearances of the Risen Savior

It is said that the Risen Savior ascended and descended many times, even after the Great Ascension and Pentecost. Thus, the Risen Savior continued to appear to the apostles and disciples for many years after the resurrection. Many would say that the Risen Savior continues to appear to those who desire to receive him and who desire to receive the Light-transmission.

Of those to whom the Risen Savior appeared, it is St. Mary Magdalene to whom he appeared the most. Thus she received more teachings of the Risen Savior than any other apostle. It is often said that he continued to appear until St. Michael came of age, which is to say thirteen years and nine months, during which time he revealed many mysteries to the Holy Bride.

Perhaps the latter appearances of the Living Yeshua are the same as those during the initial years following the resurrection. Yet, in those years immediately following the resurrection, the True Gospel was given to the apostles by the Risen Savior, which is a Holy Gospel beyond what appears in the Bible of the outer and unspiritual church. Indeed, the Gnostic Gospel is the Gospel of the Risen Christ, of which the Gospels that appear in the common Bible are akin to a prologue. Thus, among Gnostics, there are secret and hidden gospels, and it is said that there are gospels as yet to be revealed before the Second Coming transpires.

The Bride in the Pentecost

On the day of the Pentecost, the men and women disciples closest to the Lord were gathered in the upper room—all who had been present at the Last Supper and when the Risen Savior first appeared. The women prepared the sacred space, as at the Last Supper, and the disciples gathered in prayer and meditation. Suddenly, a great fiery light appeared over the Holy Bride. It came to rest upon her and then divided into tongues of fire, which went out and came to rest upon the heads of every disciple present, both the men and women. She was the matrix below of the fiery-light presence above, and from her it passed unto all who were present. The men were driven out of the upper room by the Holy Spirit, but the women remained in the upper room with St. Mary Magdalene. They prayed and worshipped, sang and danced, and spoke of secret mysteries in the upper room all day and long into the night. Thus the women served as the matrix and generator of the Light that the men went out to extend, and the first apostle and Holy Bride was the center of the matrix of the Light-transmission. And so she is to this very day.

The Circle of the Bride in Galilee

The men who were apostles remained in Galilee after the Pentecost. Over time, one by one, they were sent by the Holy Spirit into various lands and among various peoples. St. Mary Magdalene, however, went to the hills of Galilee. Joseph of Arimathea, along with other disciples, went with her, though, mostly, it was women who were with her. There, for some time, she taught and initiated those who came to her, and a fairly large circle of disciples gathered around her. From time to time, a few of the men who were apostles would come to visit her and to inquire of the secret teachings the Lord had given to her, as well as to listen and hear the secret Gospel the Risen Savior gave to her. St. John, St. Philip, St. Andrew, St. Thomas, and St. Jude were those who would come, and once St. James also came; but by all the other male apostles, she was shunned and rejected.

There in the hills of Galilee, she gave birth to her child. She waited until he was old enough to travel, for the Lord had said to his disciples while he lived, "When I am no longer with you, turn away from Jerusalem, for there are many archons gathered about her, and she will soon become the haunt of demons and habitation of the beasts of the field and wild creatures." This, Our Lady kept in mind, for she knew what was to come to pass in the place they put the Lord to death. Thus, she remained only a few years before departing to another distant land. While she was there, it is said she performed many wonders and taught many people the Way. Some say she lived and taught near a place called Safed, but no one truly knows where she stayed while she remained in the holy land.

The Mother and the Bride

Lady Mary and Mother Mary lived apart following the ascension of the Lord, yet in the Holy Spirit they were inseparable. Wherever the Bride was, the angel of the Mother was also present; and wherever the Mother was, there the angel of the Bride would be. To know one was to know the other; for in truth the Mother and the Bride are the same Wisdom.

Once, before the Mother's ascension, Our Lady went to visit her. No one has ever said what they spoke about or what transpired when they met, but we are told that it was akin to the Transfiguration and the Light-presence became visible to those who witnessed their meeting. Shortly thereafter, it is said that the Holy Mother departed the world without having tasted death.

Here, we may speak quite clearly: The Mother-Bride is the redemption of true womanhood. Though ignorant men may reject God the Mother and the Holy Bride, God forbid that a woman reject her own Soul and Self!

Notes

1. A Gnostic term for Light-emanations, akin to the term "Sefirot" in the Kabbalah.

2. Gospel of St. John 3:11–12.

3. Birth, Baptism, Transfiguration, Crucifixion, Resurrection, Ascension, Unification, and Enthronement are considered the eight cycles of initiation in Gnostic Christianity; hence the eightfold initiation.

4. A name for the archangel Metatron, though often used to indicate the image of Metatron and Sandalphon as one Great Angel.

5. The term "Great Seth" is often applied to the union of the Lord and the Bride.

6. Gnostic term for the rite of the Holy Eucharist.

7. Perfect Light-emanation.

8. Advanced Gnostic initiates and elders.

CYCLE 5

THE SACRED CIRCLE
OF THE BRIDE

The Guardian of the Bride

St. John became the guardian of the Holy Mother and St. Joseph of Arimathea became the guardian of the Holy Bride. Joseph was from among the Pharisees and a secret disciple of Lord Yeshua. He dearly honored and loved St. Mary Magdalene, calling her "my Lady," just as he spoke of Yeshua as "my Lord." Thus, Joseph received teachings and initiations from Lady Mary and from Lord Yeshua and was a discile to both Our Lord and Our Lady. Because of this, Lord Yeshua charged Joseph with the guardianship of the Holy Bride, and the sacred trust pleased Joseph deeply.

When the Lord departed, Joseph acquired a house for Mary in the hills of Galilee and he tended to her every need. There St. Michael grew in her womb and a circle of companions gathered around her. To anyone who would listen and hear, she taught the Gospel of Truth and she imparted teachings and initiations to every disciple according to each one's desire to receive and embody the Light-presence.

Once Mary's son was born, Joseph acquired a wet-nurse so that Lady Mary could freely teach and periodically go on retreat into the wilderness as she was inclined to do. Thus, Mary, along with women disciples, tended to St. Michael, and Joseph was like a father to him. When it came time for the Bride and St. Michael to depart the holy land, St. Joseph arranged transport and traveled with them. He was with St. Mary Magdalene and St. Michael until his death.

The Time of Departure

When the Lord was crucified on the Mount of Golgotha, the fate of Jerusalem was sealed. When he was raised up from the dead, his Body of Light became the living and eternal temple and the temple on earth was like a husk to be shed. Thus, all along, St. Mary Magdalene intended to depart from the holy land, knowing the Spirit of Holiness was no longer in it. Mary was merely waiting until St. Michael was old enough to travel a great distance. While she waited, she sought to plant seeds of Light and to establish a circle of true gnosis.

As St. Michael grew, word that Yeshua conceived a son with Mary came to the attention of the Jewish authorities. Some men among them plotted to have St. Michael found and put to death, because they feared he would acquire the power of his father and be loved by the people as Yeshua was loved. It was this that determined the time of Lady Mary's departure from the holy land, for the Risen Savior appeared to her and told her of the danger. In this way, she knew the time had come.

Mary told Joseph that the time had come, and he swiftly made preparations for the journey. Mary blessed all of her disciples and celebrated the wedding feast with them. She laid hands on a woman called Ruth, recognizing her as the elder of the circle and leaving the companions in her care. Of her circle of companions, only Salome, the young lad, and St. Joseph were allowed to travel with her and St. Michael to the new land. The rest were to remain in Galilee to extend the Light of True Gnosis. The following night, Mary, her son, and her companions set out on their journey.

The Wedding Feast of the Bride

Before Lady Mary departed her circle in Galilee, she celebrated the rite of the wedding feast with her companions. They gathered under the starry night sky and reclined at a table. Bread and wine were brought out, and Mary blessed the bread and wine, saying, "As Melchizedek brought out bread and wine and blessed Abraham and Sarah, so, now, do I bless you. Look and see the stars and reckon them, for so shall the elect be numbered and so shall they shine. As the Lord offered up his body and blood, so is this bread and wine the perfect remembrance through which you are also raised up and joined to the mystical body of the Anointed." Then she blessed the bread and wine, invoked the name of God Most High, the name of the Father and Mother and the Son and the Daughter, and all partook of the holy feast.

There was sorrow and joy among her companions, for many saw the luminous assembly of prophets, angels, and righteous spirits gather with them, and Mary imparted many secret teachings that night. Yet, they mourned the departure of their beloved mistress of Spirit, for they adored the Anointed Bride.

When midnight came, the Holy Bride arose and went to her dear disciple, Ruth. She laid her hands upon Ruth, saying, "Beloved sister, the Mother Spirit calls you to be elder of the circle, for she has established the light in you and granted you acquaintance with the Living Yeshua. You are full of Light and the Spirit and know the Way, having become the Way. Blessed are you, my little one, my sister, my mother, my grandmother; in you, there is love and knowledge, and there is understanding and wisdom. So I call you the knowledge-keeper and mother of the circle. Blessed are you, Elder Ruth, and blessed is El Elyon, Our Father and Our Mother. Amen." When Mary did this, Ruth shone with a visible light, the stars danced in the sky, and light and fire came from the Bride and entered into Ruth. She was complete and made perfect on that night. There was awe and trembling among the companions and their sorrow was turned into joy. It was a vision of great beauty. All gave thanks and praise to Yahweh, and to Our Lord and Our Lady. In this way, Lady Mary comforted her companions before she departed from them, leaving an apostle of Light among them.

The Journey

There is little said of St. Mary Magdalene's journey to the distant land, although it is said that, along the way, she stilled a violent sea and called upon the winds for a swift journey. Some have said that they stopped along the way in the land that has come to be called England, and that Mary preached the Gospel of Truth there and taught and initiated many people before completing her journey. Those who say she laid over in England also say that St. Joseph of Arimathea died and was buried there, his bones remaining in that land to this day. Others say that St. Mary Magdalene made her way straight to the new land, which has come to be known as Southern France, and that St. Joseph, along with Salome the maiden and the young lad, was with her and St. Michael when they arrived in Southern France. In any case, it was among the people of Southern France that Our Lady made her home and where she generated many circles of true gnosis.

Now, when they departed the old holy land, it is said that Lady Mary and St. Joseph carried the sacred lance and Holy Grail with them, and these holy relics remained with Lady Mary wherever she lived. Thus, ultimately, they were brought to France. Of course, the meaning of the sacred lance is the Bridegroom and the meaning of the Holy Grail is the Bride—hence, the Light and Fire of True Gnosis.

The Bride's Reception

As we know, pagan seers foretold the birth of the Holy Bride, and among the peoples of the new land there were prophecies of her coming to them and living among them—the incarnation of the Great Goddess. Thus, when Our Lady arrived and the people heard her preaching and beheld the presence and power of Christ the Sophia, they received her as a holy woman and goddess. Quite naturally, the people began to worship her, but she did not allow it. She taught them, saying, "What I am and who the Lord is, you are also; the One Life-power is in you. Worship God Most High, Our Father and Our Mother, and worship the Truth and Light in the Spirit. Do not worship or bow down to any appearance, whether in heaven above, on earth below, or beneath the earth; for the Holy One worthy of worship is the Great Spirit[1] and is invisible." This was a teaching she had to give everywhere she went. By and large, the people swiftly understood what she was saying and many became true Christians, which is to say Gnostics—knowers of Christos.

News of the arrival of St. Mary Magdalene spread swiftly in the new land. Many people came out to see her as she went from village to village, preaching the Gospel of Truth, teaching and initiating, and performing many wonders. Thus, the presence of the Holy Bride was like a wildfire spreading through the people and the land, driving out all darkness and manifesting the grace of the Spiritual Sun. There she lived and moved among the people for many years, and St. Michael after her. Thus, many call Southern France the new holy land, because the Holy Bride was received there and lived there in great joy.

The Jealous Sorcerer

In the new land, Lady Mary became well known as a holy apostle, which is to say a prophetess of God and wonder-worker.[2] People came from great distances to seek the help of the Bride, to listen to her teachings, and witness the wonders she continually performed. She helped everyone who came to her in faith and with a good heart. She taught and initiated all who desired to receive the Spirit of Truth.

Not everyone so easily received the Bride, however, for among the priests and priestesses of the old religion, many were unhappy with her presence. They felt their power among the people diminishing. However, most tolerated her presence, feeling she was a holy woman, and did not actively strive against her. There were just as many who clung to the old ways among the people as those who sought the way taught by Our Lady, and Lady Mary did not impose herself upon the people. She left each to choose for her or himself. Yet, there was a sorcerer who became sorely jealous of her. He was once considered the most powerful wonder-worker in the land and invoked dread in the people because of his inclination to dark forces. Thus, becoming angry and filled with hatred of the Bride, he sought to undermine her works of wonder. He worked his sorcery to plague anyone he heard of who had been helped by Our Lady. All of his efforts came to nothing, and this kindled his rage even more.

One night, while he slept, an angel of the Lord came to him in his dreams and warned the sorcerer not to strike out at the sons and daughters of the Light. Nevertheless, in spite of this, he continued to invoke the works of pain and hatred. Then, the Risen Savior appeared to him in a vision, and said to him, "Look and see the One you are persecuting, and behold your own undoing!" The sorcerer saw his own death, but he thought it was merely an enchantment cast by

Lady Mary to frighten him. Falling into even greater rage and darkness, he cast a spell of destruction, seeking to steal the soul of Our
Lady. Then, the angel of Our Lady appeared to the sorcerer and gave
the soul of Our Lady to him. The soul of Our Lady became a great
Light-presence enshrouding him, but to him it was as the fire of
Gehenna and it completely devoured him, so that he was burnt to
death. Casting his unholy spell, he invoked judgment upon himself.
In truth, Our Lady merely gave him what he invoked, namely her
holy soul, which is the Christos.

The next morning the sorcerer's young apprentice found him dead.
He became terrified, for he knew what his master had been doing.
The apprentice went to Lady Mary in fear, seeking her forgiveness.
He came to Lady Mary, trembling as he approached her, and said to
her, "Mistress, my master is dead. Please forgive me for my evil." Mary
reached out and touched him, and a demon departed from him. Then
she said to him, "Child, you are forgiven. Turn away from the darkness and come into the Light. Go and do for everyone what you
would have them do for you—live by way of love."

News of this went out in the land, and no one sought to challenge
Lady Mary by dark arts again. It is said that those who practiced the
dark arts departed the land, and only those of the old religion remained who were not inclined to the path of darkness.

The World of Spirits

Lady Mary was in a village giving teachings, and a man said to her,
"My Lady, you speak of the Lord of Spirits and the play of spirits in the
world, both spirits of light and spirits of darkness. Yet, these do not appear to us in the world. Where do these spirits dwell?" She said to him,
"My brother, the world of spirits is hidden within and behind the
world that appears, and it is veiled by the appearances of this world.
The spirits play in the hearts and minds of human beings, some seeking good, some evil. Many are neither good nor evil, but something
admixed. To know the Lord of Spirits is to gain discernment of the
spirits and to no longer be bound to the play of spirits. The Anointed
is the Lord of Spirits, for he was raised up in a spiritual body and as-

cended into the Supernal Abode." Then the man asked Mary, "Knowing the Lord of Spirits, do we invoke spirits?" She said to him, "We are no longer the slaves of the archons or the spirits. Yet, truly, we do invoke the spirits, for we are to impart the Spirit of Truth to visible and invisible spirits so that all might be uplifted in the body of the Human One." He said to her, "How can we believe in and invoke what we do not see?" She said to him, "We speak of love and we love, but no one has ever seen love. It is the same in spiritual things. Yet, when one awakens, they can see. It is only while we sleep that we cannot see because our eyes are closed. Pray to the Lord of Spirits to awaken you!"

The Healing of Womanhood

A woman came to Mary seeking healing. The woman said to her, "Beloved Mistress, I suffer pain in my body and I have become addle-headed, so that my memory fails me. I have been to the healers and none have been able to help me. Please, my Lady, heal me." Lady Mary said to her, "This pain is in the soul and the mind, not in the body, though the mind puts it into the body. You reject the body because it is a female body, and because of this pain, you are not responsible for yourself. It is not a healing you need, my sister, but an exorcism, for this is a creature of pain and hatred you have taken into yourself."

Lady Mary put her hand on the woman's head, and said, "Out!" The woman fell to the ground as the evil spirit departed her. Then Mary put her hand on the woman's heart. She called upon the name of the Lord and the Mother Spirit, and said, "Come in!" and the woman's soul was restored to her. When the woman opened her eyes, she beheld the Light-image of the Mother with Mary, and she saw Mary radiant with light and glory. Mary said to the woman, "Behold, my sister, the true image of womanhood and remember yourself in God. Embrace your holy soul and the sacredness of your womanhood."

Our Lady exorcised such demons from many women, sometimes merely by her presence, showing the women the image of true womanhood and imparting gnosis of Christ the Sophia in woman's form. It was a spiritual healing of womanhood, and the Spirit of the Bride continues this labor of healing to this very day among us.

The Village of Lepers

Our Lady was walking in the countryside. A man ran up to her to warn her of a village of lepers ahead. He was hunting in the forest and saw that she was going toward it. She said to the man, "These are children of Our Mother too, and such as these are dear to her." The man was bewildered. He followed behind her, wondering who she was and what she was doing. She walked into the village and, as she did, all who were in the village were healed. They felt the power of God come upon them and great warmth in their bodies. Then a great shout went up from the village, for the people were overwhelmed by joy.

Now the man did not know what had happened. He saw all of the people throng around Lady Mary and saw them touching her. It appeared to him as though they were killing her; so he fled to his village to tell his people of what he had seen. His fear and hatred of lepers clouded his mind.

The men of his village decided to go out and kill the lepers for their alleged crime, but when they arrived at the lepers' village, they found all the lepers healed and Mary sitting and teaching them. The man said to Mary, "I did not know you were a holy woman. I have never seen such a thing. How can this be?" She said to him, "A great Light has come into the world and many wonders are coming to pass. What has never been seen is now openly being revealed. Come with your friends; sit down and listen." So the man and the others who were with him sat down and Mary taught them of the Way.

When Mary finished teaching, the man invited her and those who were healed by her to his village. He wanted his people to see and to hear the Gospel themselves and to be filled with joy as he was filled with joy. He and those who were with him believed in the Anointed and sought to become acquainted. So Mary and those who were healed went with the men to their village. Mary healed others among the villagers, taught them the Gospel of Truth and the threefold initiation,[3] and a great feast was celebrated.

It is said that spontaneous healings were not uncommon in the presence of the Holy Bride. Many times, she merely walked among those who were ill and they were healed of their disease. Because of this, many came to have faith in the Anointed and the Bride and many acquired gnosis because they first had faith.

Lady of the Woods and Mistress of Wild Things

In the new land, Lady Mary loved to go into the woods for prayer and meditation, just as, in the holy land, she enjoyed retreats into the wilderness of the desert. One time, a young disciple followed her into the woods, wishing to be near her and to see what she was doing. When she passed through a clearing and went into the tree line on the other side, the disciple lost sight of her. He ran to catch up, but just as he entered among the trees he found himself surrounded by a pack of wolves, each wolf staring at him in silence. He was frozen with fear and did not dare move for fear the wolves would swiftly be upon him. Then Lady Mary appeared and said to him, "I did not ask for your company. Why are you following me?" He responded, saying, "My Lady, I only sought to be near you and to see what you were doing." She said to him, "It is dangerous to draw near to a queen without the permission of the king or of the queen herself, for her guards are likely to kill a man intruding upon her privacy. I go out to meet with my Beloved and it is a private matter. It is unbecoming that you have followed me. Return to your place, and do not go out or come in unless the Spirit of the Lord moves you." Having said this, Lady Mary vanished into the woods. The wolves vanished with her, leaving the young man in awe. Needless to say, the young disciple never followed Our Lady into the woods again.

There were many times disciples saw wolves going along with the Holy Bride in the woods, as well as other wild beasts. When she was in the holy land and would go out into the desert, it is said that lions and leopards and all manner of wild things would draw near to her when she prayed and meditated, never causing her any harm. It always seemed that wild things loved our Lady and communed with her. There were so many stories of people seeing wild creatures with Our Lady in the woods that many called her the Lady of the Forest;

others called her the Mistress of Wild Things and sometimes Lady of the Beasts.

Our Lady Preaching

Lady Mary did not only teach human beings. She also taught the Gospel to animals, trees, and the wilderness itself. As much as she preached the Gospel to visible spirits, she also instructed invisible spirits in the Gospel. Through her, the Light of Truth was extended to all spirits and creatures who desired to receive it. Thus, she taught her disciples to do likewise, so that they might know the wonders of Sophia and entertain the communion of Our Earthly Mother. She said to her disciples, "If the Light of Our Heavenly Father is not brought down into Our Earthly Mother, to be received by all her children, then the Second Coming of Christ will not transpire in the world."

A young man once came into the company of Lady Mary and sought to become a disciple after hearing her give teachings. The eloquence of her teachings on the prophets and the Gospel, along with her beauty, attracted him. He was baptized, anointed, and celebrated the rite of the wedding feast. After a few days, however, he became disturbed. He saw Mary talking with invisible spirits, but assumed she was talking to herself. He also watched her talk to birds and to trees, even to rocks. So he wondered if she was mad or if she might be possessed by some strange spirit. He did not say anything but he departed her company, not intending to return.

He walked for some distance. As he was passing through some trees, a flight of crows landed in them. They began chattering among themselves, as crows tend to do, and cawing back and forth. He smiled, thinking of Lady Mary and how silly she was. Just then, however, he realized that the crows were speaking the Gospel and he could understand everything they were saying, much to his complete astonishment! He was amazed and went straight back to Lady Mary.

When the young man arrived, Lady Mary was teaching some disciples. She looked up and smiled at him. She said to him, "Today crows instructed a human being in the wisdom of the Gospel and bore witness of the Anointed Bride. Yet, it is the human being who is meant to tend and instruct all God's creatures and draw them in ascent. Let us pray that creation is rightly ordered and illuminated by the holy name of God that only a human being can speak." Then she led the disciples in prayer and the young man joined in with them. From that day on, he was a true and faithful disciple of Our Lady.

It was often like this with Our Lady; many at first would think she was silly, only to discover she was very wise!

Wisdom of Herbs and Flowers

Lady Mary was noted for her knowledge of herbs and flowers and such things, and for the knowledge of how to make potions and ointments and the like for various ailments. A young woman disciple found this curious because she knew Mary had a great healing power and did not need such things to heal. So she asked Mary, "Mistress, why do you make concoctions for healing when you have the power to heal without them?" Mary said, "Dear child, it is not given that everyone can be healed directly by God's Spirit, for to many it is not possible. But, given something visible as a talisman of healing and believing it will help them, many are relieved in this way. Love seeks to comfort and heal in any way possible. Do not discount the Sophia of Our Earthly Mother because you know the Sophia of Our Heavenly Father; for the wisdom of heaven and earth are one and the same—the Holy Spirit."

It is said that Lady Mary taught many disciples the healing way, both of the Spirit that comes from within and above, and the Spirit that comes from within and below.

Invocation of Azrael

A disciple of Mary's came to her and said, "Mistress, I seek freedom from bondage." Mary said to her, "If that is your heart's wish, then when the new moon comes, go to a place of graves at night and lay yourself down. Invoke Brother Azrael[4] and meditate on death. Envision yourself as a corpse in the grave and your body devoured in the grave over the ages, until nothing remains but earth. When you have done this and you have an intimate acquaintance with Brother Azrael, come and see me."

The woman did as Mary instructed her, fasting and praying until the new moon and then seeking knowledge of death. When she returned to Mary and reported what transpired, Mary said to her, "In the remembrance of death, live and love the Lord of Life; abide always in joy, so that the Holy Shekinah is your constant companion. With the joy of life, surrender yourself to the cross and you will not taste death." Then she taught the woman the feast of perfect delight and transference of the soul. The woman practiced these for years. When she eventually died, it is said she left no body behind.

Three Women and the Sacred Tree

Lady Mary taught many sacred ceremonies, for she found them helpful to many of her companions seeking gnosis. One ceremony she taught for extending blessings involved a virgin, a mother, an elderly woman, and a sacred tree. The women would go out on the full moon. All three would touch the tree and invoke God the Mother, and the light of the moon and stars would come down into the tree. Anyone who cleaved in their heart to the Mother and Bride and touched the tree would be blessed, as would anyone whose name was spoken while touching the tree. In this way, Our Lady taught a ceremony of divine grace through which many among the faithful received blessings.

The Circle of Our Lady

Lady Mary generated a large circle of disciples in the new land. In due time, she had recognized and ordained many apostles and elders, so that many circles of true gnosis arose. It was a great matrix of Light. The circle of Our Lady was at the center, and many circles were gathered around it. Lady Mary would travel from circle to circle, and when she was with her own circle, there was a constant coming and going of apostles and disciples. She taught and initiated thousands of faithful and elect into the Way.

Among her disciples, there were men and women, and so also among the apostles and elders. Like Lord Yeshua, she gave outer and public teachings good for everyone, but to her disciples she gave inner and secret teachings in private. Thus, outwardly, assemblies of the faithful formed, but inwardly there was an assembly of the elect. There was an outer and an inner church, and a secret order within the interior church. Over time, this gave rise to several lineages of the Light-transmission, each lineage having its root in the lineage of Our Lady. Truly, Our Lady was a great Light-bearer and holy apostle. It is said that some of these lineages continue to this day.

The Spirit Jar

A disciple of Our Lady found a jar while meditating in a cave. It had elaborate carvings upon it. He thought it might contain gold or some other precious thing, and seeing its beauty, he took the jar with him. As an act of devotion to his holy tzaddik, he offered the beautiful jar to Lady Mary. When he drew near her to present her with the jar, Mary said to him, "What have you done? There is a powerful evil bound in that jar. Had you opened that jar or it fell from your hands, the great demon bound within it would have destroyed you! One should never take possession of such objects found in caves or buried in the wilderness, save by way of a word of knowledge given by the Mother Spirit who reveals wisdom treasuries that are meant to be discovered. Go and return this jar to where you found it. Bury it so no one else might see it." The disciple swiftly followed her instructions.

When the disciple returned, Mary thought it best to teach him about spirit jars and spirit traps and how they are consecrated and used. She also taught him the way of the sacred quest for wisdom treasuries. This was Mary's way; she always corrected error with knowledge. Though at times she could be very severe, she was also extremely generous, kind, and compassionate with teachings. Many secret things, such as these, Lady Mary learned from Lord Yeshua, for among other things, he had full knowledge of the wonder-working arts. As much as a prophet, he was also a great wonder-worker.

A Young Man Seeking Wealth

It was not uncommon, on some occasions, for Lady Mary to grant blessings for prosperity, among other things. Thus, a young man came to her who sought wealth. He was infatuated with her and knew of her wonder-working power. So he approached her and said, "I know that God is with you and that you can grant any blessing you wish. I come seeking a blessing." Mary inquired, "Have you asked the Lord in prayer to give to you what you are seeking? For if you have faith and are acquainted, the Spirit of the Lord will do whatever you ask and she will give you all that you seek to receive." "Yes, my Lady, I have prayed to become a wealthy man, and receiving wealth I have vowed to tend to orphans, widows, and the poor, and to support elders and apostles of the Way." Mary then taught him everything the Lord spoke about wealth, but the man remained stubborn to his desire for it. Mary said to him, "God intends you to have everything good, even wealth, if that is your heart's desire. Come with me and I will grant this boon."

Lady Mary took a sword; she had the young man carry her staff, and she led him out into the woods. Once there she traced a circle on the ground and invoked the Great Name of God. Then she called the young man into the circle and told him to lay the staff on the ground. When he did this, she ran him through with the sword, killing him. Then she drove the sword into the earth and picked up her staff. She called the man's soul back into him and healed his wound. She said to him, "This evening you are born under lucky stars, and now you can gather in all the wealth you desire, for you have risen to a new life this evening!"

Now while the young man was dead, he saw a vision of the Risen Savior and the Supernal Abode, and he knew all the wealth in this world as nothing compared to the glory of the World of Supernal Light. He said to Mary, "That is no longer my desire, for I have seen the Living One!" But Mary said to him, "How wonderful! Yet, it shall come to pass that great wealth pours upon you. So, if you like, keep it or give it all away, as you wish! Power is power on earth or in heaven, and there is nothing good or evil about it. It is what is in the heart and mind of a person that determines what any power is. In ignorance, most become intoxicated and forget to serve the kingdom with their life's blood and power. But you are no longer ignorant. Therefore, be sober and trust in the Spirit of Yahweh!"

As it turned out, as though by magic, wealth came to the lad. He could hardly give it away fast enough. With his wealth, he remained faithful to the Lord and to Our Lady, and he served the Divine Kingdom well. As a matter of fact, he brought many wealthy people into the acquaintance of the Lord and the Holy Bride, who also served the great work in the new land.

Miracles

Lady Mary was teaching people in the countryside, for she was not inclined to go into the cities. Many people were coming out to see her and to listen to her teachings, for they had never heard anyone speak with such presence and authority, and Yahweh and the Anointed were unknown to them. When Mary taught, she would also banish unclean and dark spirits from people and heal people and many signs of wonders happened.

Mary was teaching outside a town and a woman said to her, "Holy One, miracles were few before you came among us, but now they are abundant. Even your companions perform wonders!" Mary said to her, "Miracles are few because there are few who have faith and know the light that is in them, and few understand that they are part of the miracles they seek. You marvel at wonders, but do not know the power of God in you and that you are sons and daughters of the Most High. If your heart is good and your mind is clear and you cleave to the Anointed who dwells in you, nothing will be impossible to you. Have faith and seek acquaintance."

A Dangerous Friend

A woman said to Mary, "You speak often of the Lord, Yeshua Messiah. Please tell us what the Lord was like." Mary said, "He was the most wonderful and dangerous friend! He was like unto no man. He was

natural and spontaneous, completely uncontrived, and therefore completely unpredictable. He was fluid and flowing, and yet unmovable.
He was ecstatic and wild and fierce, and yet the most gentle and compassionate of souls. It was impossible to manipulate him, because he
followed the Holy Spirit and did what he saw the Living Father
doing. He was who he was, and no other. He was a little boy, a man
and an old man, the image of true manhood. He was filled with Light,
was on fire with the Spirit of Yahweh, and he set the world on fire!
The Lord was a prophet and a wonder-worker, and a delightful story-
teller. He would do anything he needed to do to illuminate souls and
to liberate them, even unto death on the cross."

Then the woman asked Mary, "But why do you call him dangerous?" Mary said, "Because he was a revolutionary and adversary to the
religious establishment. He sought to turn your world upside down
and to lead into the mystical death through which rebirth in the
Mother Spirit comes to pass. If one clung to one's life or to the world,
he was truly dangerous. He sought to drive people mad with divine
passion, as do I."

A Perfect Lover

A disciple of Lady Mary once asked her, "Who was Lord Yeshua?"
Mary answered her, saying, "He was the perfect lover, my sister, like
no other. At a mere glance, he could send the soul into ecstasy, and
with just a touch, he could thrill the heart. His kisses set one's body
on fire, and his embrace was the sweet dissolution of all, so that nothing remained save the Beloved! He was awesome and wonderful! He
made love to the Soul of the World to bring forth new life, and his
love never failed to bring the perfection of delight. He was the fulfillment of every man and woman and creature of God, and he taught us
all how to love and how to be human beings."

The Lady

A young woman came among the companions of Our Lady while she
was giving teachings openly. She said to Mary, "My Lady, I wish to
become your disciple, for I see that there is divinity in you and know

you are a woman of God." Mary responded, saying, "That is well and good, but I am not your Lady. I am the Lady of those who love the Lord and who are received by the Lord, those who have intimate knowledge of the Mother Spirit. It is the Holy Spirit who is Our Lady and the Christos who is Our Lord. The Lord is not Yeshua and the Lady is not Mary, but Our Lord and Our Lady are the Light and Fire in you." Then Mary charged two of her companions to baptize and anoint the young woman, and when she was received there was a wedding feast.

After the holy feast, the young woman said to Lady Mary, "Please Mistress, allow me to go to my husband and bring him also." Mary said, "As you wish, my sister." So the young woman went to her husband and said to him, "I have met the woman of Light, who has revealed everything to me. Come and meet her!" So the young man went and he met Lady Mary, and he also received the Spirit of Truth and was received into the company of heaven. Mary said to the young woman, "There is light within you and it is good, and today you have fulfilled Eve."

The Anointed Bride

St. Mary Magdalene set many on the path and she preached the Gospel of the Risen Savior openly. She did not receive everyone who came to her as a disciple—only those given to her by the Mother Spirit and who had a heart connection with her. To those she received she revealed the Anointed Bride, but among the multitude she walked as a holy woman and wonder-worker.

One evening she was among her close companions. One of her disciples inquired of the Transfiguration and the true nature of the Bride. She said to Mary, "Holy Lady, we know you are the Holy Bride and the Daughter of the Mother Spirit. We bow down before God the Mother and the Living Father, and before the Spiritual Sun and Holy Spirit, and we give all praise to God Most High. We yearn to know you in all of your forms, and to know the One Anointed with the Supernal Light of God. Please, Beloved Mistress, show us yourself, that we might see and hear and know, and thus bear true witness."

Mary said, "Look and see." All who were present found their own bodies becoming radiant and everything around them becoming light. Light-images of the Transfiguration of the Anointed Bride appeared, and she revealed to them the seven faces of the Holy Bride. Light-images of the Maiden of Light, the Mother of Royal Blood, and Grandmother Wisdom appeared. Images of the Radiant Darkness, Lilith, Naamah, and Iggaret[5] appeared. The Anointed Bride was all of these, and yet the image of Clear Light beyond all images. The body of Mary became translucent light, as though a rainbow in the sky, and then transparent light. When she reappeared, her companions sat thunderstruck, filled with holy awe and wonder.

The disciple who invoked the revelation of the Bride spoke and said, "Anointed Lady, in you the light and darkness are joined, and there is perfect being, perfect intelligence, and perfect delight. Truly, you are the Daughter of the Great Mother!" Mary said, "What I am, so also are you. You have beheld the Truth of the Soul of Light in you. Remember yourselves, and you shall be as I am." Then Mary gave teachings on Eve and Lilith and the Woman of Light. When Mary completed the transmission, Mary and her companions celebrated a great feast. They sang and danced in the presence of Yahweh, rejoicing in life abundant and their freedom.

When the evening passed, Mary said to her companions, "Unless a person already knows, having looked and seen, listened and heard, do not speak of what the Mother Spirit has shown you. Such things are given unto souls in due season, and each soul must ripen before being harvested. The Lord said, 'Many are called, but few are so chosen.'"

The Wicked Disciple

Lady Mary Magdalene preached the Gospel of Truth, and she taught her disciples the outer, inner, and secret mysteries, the way of the work of creation, and the way of the chariot of Ascension. Thus she taught the path of the prophets and path of the initiates. Everything the Lord taught to her and revealed to her she gave to her close disciples, including all knowledge of the wonder-working art.

Although the true wonder-working art is in the soul and in the mind and heart, she also taught her disciples the outer ways through which the mind, heart, and life might be consecrated and the power of the Holy Spirit might become known. Thus she taught circle drawing, altar building, how to make fetishes and talismans, among other things. Everything she taught was for the worship of God in Spirit and Truth and for the sake of blessing the people.

One of the women she taught the blessing ways secretly began performing the wonder-working art for money. She began to act as a fortuneteller, to put herself off as a prophetess, and to cast spells for people—akin to the way of sorcery, seeking to profit from spiritual gifts. At one point, she fell into great darkness and used her knowledge for a wealthy man to murder his enemy. She made a wax figure of the man's enemy and carved the signs upon it, not to bless but to curse. On account of this, the man's enemy died. Lady Mary became aware of what her disciple was doing, for the Mother Spirit revealed it to Mary. So Mary sent two disciples to fetch the woman.

While the disciples were getting the woman to bring her to Mary, Lady Mary prepared an altar and she made a wax figure of a woman, placing the signs of justice upon it, and she laid it upon the altar. Then, she sat waiting for the woman. When the woman arrived, Mary said to her, "Look at what you have done!" The woman looked and saw the altar and the figure upon it, and the Holy Spirit struck her down so that she fell dead. Several disciples then took the woman's body away and buried it.

When the disciples returned, one of them said to her, "Blessed Lady, you have slain an evil-doer and what you have done is justice." Mary said, "I have done nothing. It is the Holy Spirit that has done this, not I, but the Mother Spirit. This woman has brought about her own destruction, for such is the nature of evil—it is self-destructive."

A Broken Person

A disciple of Lady Mary cast a powerful evil spirit out of a man. Afterward, he wished to be a disciple to Mary. Thus, Mary's disciple brought the man to her. Mary was in her house giving teachings. The disciple told the man to wait outside, and then the disciple entered into the house. Mary greeted her, saying, "Peace, my sister." The woman responded, "Peace, my Lady. I have brought someone to meet you. He had a powerful demon in him and through the power of the Mother Spirit, it was cast out of him. Having become clean, he wishes to be set on the path and has asked to be your disciple." Mary said to her, "This cannot be, for he is a broken vessel, and his mending will not come in this life. It will come in a future life, and then, perhaps, we will meet again. Go and tell him to live by what is right and true and to love deeply and to worship God according to his understanding. That is enough for him."

Mary turned to her disciples and said, "When a pot has been fired, but then fractures or breaks, it cannot be remolded. A new pot must be fashioned in order for a proper vessel to be formed."

The Omen of Death

It was late in the evening and Lady Mary was in a house to which she was invited for dinner. After the meal, those who were in attendance had many questions, and she was answering them and instructing them in the Way. While she was teaching, an owl flew into the house and alighted on the table. Some of the women screamed, "God! No! Someone is going to die!" Their tumult sent the owl straight out of the house. Mary stood up and spoke sharply. She rebuked them, saying, "Look at what you have done! You profane the name of God and defile the sacred circle, and you have chased the blessing of the Holy Mother out of the house! Do you not understand that you must die to be reborn of the Mother Spirit? This was an omen of new life, not death. And why do you fear death? It is merely the passage of the soul of Light from a husk of darkness, for truly, as the Lord lives, death has never existed." Mary then swiftly departed the house, leaving the women to consider her words, and the disciples with her also departed in silence.

Fertility

A woman came to the Bride, seeking a blessing. The woman was barren and could not conceive a child. Mary had compassion on her, put her hand on the woman's belly, and blessed her, saying, "Elohim bless, Ama Aima[6] bless; Yahweh bless; in the name of El Elyon and the Mother Spirit be blessed. In the blessed name of the Anointed, you shall conceive and birth a child."

Mary took the woman into a room with several of her disciples, and they performed a name changing ceremony. Then Mary charged two of her disciples to go out, baptize the woman, anoint her, and to celebrate the wedding feast with her. This they did. In so doing, the woman was born to a new life and her holy soul was brought into her.

When the disciples had done this, they returned with the woman. Mary said to her, "Today you are a new woman, and from the bridal chamber you are blessed. Trust in Yahweh and the Mother Spirit, and what has been spoken will come to pass—amen." Many women were blessed and healed in this way by Lady Mary, and all who received her blessing bore strong and healthy children.

The Father, the Mother

Lady Mary freely taught the Gospel of Truth. She taught of the Living Father and the Divine Mother, and she taught of the Resurrection and the Holy Spirit. She taught the path of mystical prayer and prophetic meditation, and she taught the people how to make sacred rituals to celebrate the Divine Life. To the simple, she taught simple things; to those able to receive the more subtle and sublime things, she taught the more subtle and sublime. She gave to everyone what was good for them, as a mother to her children and as a bride to her husband. Always she knew what was good to give, because she gave as she saw the Holy Mother give and she moved with the Mother Spirit.

Children of Light

Lady Mary was teaching one day, and she said, "Every man is the Bridegroom and every woman is the Holy Bride, and the Beloved is the Great Spirit, to which we are all joined. The Spiritual Sun shines within everyone, only, in many, darkness and admixture obscure it. Purify your heart and mind, and the light will shine from within you as the sun shines in a clear sky, for you are children of the Light."

The Dark Mountain

There was a mountain noted as a haunt of demons and there was a poor village nearby plagued by ill fortune. On hearing of this place and the plight of the people living near it, Mary was moved with love and compassion for the people. She brought Salome with her, and they traveled to this dark abode, preaching the Risen Savior along the way, as they passed from town to town. Along the way, Mary and Salome would perform the feast of perfect delight in secret at midnight.

As she drew near the place of darkness, men of a town close to this village heard where she was going and they decided to follow along. They thought the Holy Bride and Salome needed their protection, although, indeed, they did not need protection from any man. Thus Our Lady turned them away, and refused to let them come with her and Salome.

When Our Lady arrived at the dark mountain, she did not go into the nearby village, nor did she let anyone see her and Salome. Straightaway, they climbed the mountain. When night came and the demons came out, she performed the threefold feast of perfect delight and the corresponding rite of oath-binding spirits.[7] Thus, in one night, she subjugated all the dark spirits by appeasement and oath-binding. Those that would not be appeased and oath-bound, Mary and Salome devoured and spit out into the pit, binding them completely from the earth-sphere. Then, Lady Mary invoked the divine powers and blessed the mountain.

When morning came, Mary went into the village and cast out whatever unclean and evil spirits remained in the people. She healed the sick and taught the Way of Truth. Many received the Way of

Truth, for they saw the Light-presence in Mary. The people rejoiced in their deliverance. They knew what she had done for them, and ill fortune departed the village.

Word of this spread throughout the land, and there were many towns and villages that called upon the Bride to come and subjugate dark and hostile spirits. It is said that Mary went throughout the land, subjugating dark spirits, either by oath-binding or banishing them.

Little Children

Like the Lord, Our Lady adored little children. People would often bring their children to Lady Mary so that she might bless them. Yet, Mary would often say, "I am blessed by the little children." One day, a disciple asked Mary, "When you bless children, why do you always say that they bless you?" Mary said, "Life is a blessing, and children are a bundle of life. To be able to bless others is a blessing, and one is blessed in doing it. Though no one is born enlightened, the souls of little children are nearer to the Mother Spirit. Often, little ones speak great mysteries of wisdom. It is for all of these reasons I say this. Pray to be a blessing always!"

The Healing Spring

St. Mary Magdalene was sitting near a spring known for its healing power. There were luminous spirits there, so she liked to go to it sometimes to pray and meditate in private. One day while she was there sitting alone, three lepers came, seeking healing. When they saw someone sitting nearby the spring, they began to retreat into the forest, for lepers were forbidden to draw close to people.

Seeing them, Mary called out to them, "Come, friends, seek your healing!" The lepers drew close to the spring and began putting the water from the spring upon their bodies. Mary said, "How long have you been applying the healing waters to your bodies?" One of the lepers said, "We have been here seven days now, and every day we come for the water." She asked him, "Has there been any improvement?" He said, "No, the spirits have not seen fit to give us our healing."

Mary said, "The gods and goddesses that abound, and all spirits, are subject unto the Lord of Spirits, El Elyon, and all are subject unto the Anointed and to the Holy Bride. The healing power does not come from spirits nor from these waters; it comes from the Supernal Abode of God." Mary rose up and drew near to the lepers, and she said, "Do you wish to be whole, my brothers and sister?" They answered, "Yes, we long to be healed." So Mary laid hands on them and she blessed them. In that very moment, they were healed and made whole.

The three lepers fell down upon their knees and began to worship Mary, but she said to them, "Get up and do not worship me. Give praise to God Most High and to the Spirit of the Anointed. It is God's Spirit that has healed you, and it is your faith that has made you whole. Do not worship any appearance. Worship the Holy One, who is invisible, in Spirit and Truth. What you have received, go out and give. God has put the healing power in you today." The lepers departed, leaping and laughing, and filled with the Spirit. They praised and gave thanks to God as they went along their way. It is said that they served the kingdom the remainder of their lives and that many were healed by these three.

A Blind Child

Mary was going from place to place, preaching the Living One and ministering to the needs of the people. In one village, the parents of a blind girl brought their daughter to Mary. They said to Mary, "Dear woman of God, please heal our daughter. She was born blind, and we pray that she might see." Mary laid hands on the girl, embraced her, and she inwardly prayed over her, and sight was given to the little girl. She looked at the girl and said to her, "In your last life you were called to be a seer, but you withheld yourself from your holy soul and the Mother Spirit. Now, again, it seems that you are called by the Holy Spirit. May you be true to yourself and follow the Spirit."

It was the custom among the people to give gifted children to the custody of wise men and women, especially when the blessing of a great healing was received or the preservation of life. Thus, the parents of the little girl said to Mary, "Holy woman of God, let our daughter become your daughter, so that she might walk in the path of those who see in the light." Mary said, "I receive her as my own in the blessed name of the Anointed." She said to the little girl, "Come, my daughter, we must be going." The little girl went with Mary and did not look back. It is said she became an apostle of Light and that she was a noted prophetess of God.

The Empty Woman

A woman came to Mary and said, "Mistress, from my youth I have felt hollow inside, and though I have given birth, I continue to feel empty. Sorrow plagues me and I cannot escape it. Tell me, what should I do?" Mary said, "Truly, my sister, this is true. We are empty, and we cannot be fulfilled by the favors of men, nor can we be satisfied by anything of this world. Yet, because we are empty, we can be Spirit-filled. Look deeply into this emptiness and embrace it. You will discover it is the Divine Pleroma."[8] Then Mary taught the woman the way of mystical prayer, and how to look and see. This woman was known as Rachel, and she became a dear companion to Our Lady.

Appearances

One day a man came to St. Mary Magdalene's home. He had traveled three days to see her and arrived in the midst of prayer among the companions. Mary departed from prayer to greet him. He said, "Mistress, my son lies near death. It may be that he already has died, but if he is living, if you are willing, please come and heal my boy." Mary said, "What you ask, my brother, is happening now as we speak. Your son lives and he is well. Go, return to your family and give praise and glory to the Living One." The man thanked Lady Mary' and set off for home.

When he arrived in his village, people were coming out to greet him. They told him that the Holy Bride had come and that she had raised his boy from death. The boy had died. She walked into the village and went to his home. She laid herself upon the boy and breathed his soul into him once more. The time this all transpired was the same as when he, himself, was speaking with Lady Mary, three days' journey away. He was astonished and told everyone of his experience. Many in that village came to believe in the Anointed, and those who believed sought to become acquainted.

It was reported that many times there were multiple appearances of Our Lady, each seemingly in the body. It has been said that Our Lady emanated herself to distant lands to teach the Gospel of Truth among various peoples, always in a woman's form.

The Interior Fire

Winter in the new land was very cold and there was much snow. Nevertheless, Lady Mary often enjoyed going out into the woods to pray and meditate, even in the midst of winter. She would sit, gather herself inward, and uplift her spirit to the Lord. She needed no fire to stay warm, because there was an interior fire in her. So fiery was she inwardly that snow around her was known to melt, and when it snowed, there would be none upon her body while she sat in prayer and meditation.

Once there was a disciple, new to Our Lady, who knew she had gone out to pray and meditate, and he saw that it had begun to snow. So he took her cloak and a blanket out to her. He was amazed to find her sitting on the earth and the snow melted around her. There she was, completely dry and unaffected by the snow and cold. When he drew close to her, it was as though he stood near a fire. He did not disturb her, but withdrew and went to pray, though near the warmth of the hearth in the house.

It is said that Lady Mary taught this method of holy prayer and meditation to some of her disciples for the sake of inner purification.

Travels

It was well known that Our Lady could move swiftly, much to the astonishment of others. At times, when she would travel she would go along at an ordinary pace, but at other times, she would cover great distances swiftly, as though by magic. Others traveling with her on occasions of speedy travel would say that they had walked like on any other occasion, only in a short time they would arrive at a distant place that, even on a horse, could not be reached so fast. Once a disciple inquired about this with Mary, and she simply said, "Things are not as they seem, everything is inward."

Matchmaking

Among the many things the Bride was called, one of them was the matchmaker because of her teachings on soul mates and her capacity to see links between souls. There were many couples who owed their union to the Holy Bride. When she saw connections between souls, even if the two were not soul mates, she would direct them to one another. She did not do this all of the time, only when the Mother Spirit revealed the need for two souls to come together. This same knowing allowed her to see those for whom it would be good to become disciples and those for whom it was best that they did not draw so close. It is said that she could see into souls so deeply, that she even saw into past and future lives and knew the tikkune[9] of all whom she met. Thus, she was a true teacher and guide in the Spirit.

The Old Hag

There was one reason for which Magdalene would draw close to cities. She was always something of a trickster and prankster in her way and loved giving secret blessings. Sometimes, she would turn herself into an old hag and beg at the gates of a city or in the center of a town. Whoever gave coins to her or food or drink, she would bless them secretly, and they would receive something they desired.

One day she was out playing in this way, and on that day she had received nothing. However, there was a lame man nearby who had received some bread. Seeing this old and decrepit woman, he called her over and said to her, "Grandmother, here is some bread for you. Be well." Mary, who was this old woman, said, "Bless you, my son. Be well." Some time later, he discovered he was no longer lame, and he was certain the old woman had something to do with it. Thus, he went in search of her.

Day after day he would go back to the city gate where he saw her, but he could not find her. Then he began to search the land, inquiring of all who he met about her, telling them what this old woman had done. One day he was walking along a trail in the woods, and there was the old woman. He said to her, "Grandmother! I found you! Please come, I want to care for you as you cared for me." Then Magdalene became herself, and he recognized who she was because of her presence and beauty. He said, "My Lady, you are the woman of God so many people speak about. I have longed to meet you but could not come out to see you because I was lame and there was no one to bring me. Please, may I walk with you? Truly, you are a holy woman of God, and there is nothing I desire more than to know the Way." Mary said to him, "My brother, you fed me when I was hungry, and you sought me and followed after me. Already you are a true and faithful disciple to me. Come, continue to follow and I will take you into the presence of the Living One." It is said that this man was among those who followed the Bride throughout his life, even when she departed the world.

Mary was noted for shape-shifting, much as the Risen Savior changed appearances as he liked. Many witnessed this power with her. Some even claim she could assume the forms of animals as well. Someone once asked her about this talent, and she said, "It is for the Bride to teach that one never knows when one is meeting a holy person or an angel. Many are the holy beings that secretly live and move among us, and Christ is within everyone and everything. It is the lesson of love and compassion."

The Joyful Widow

One evening Mary was giving teachings among some women, and one of them said to her, "How painful it must be to become a widow so early in life; my heart feels for you." Mary said, "Dear sister, if I am a widow, it is in joy; for the Supernal Light has come into the world, and in my heart and soul, the Anointed abides. Yet, truly I say to you, my Beloved lives and is alive—he is the Living One, the Risen Savior. He is with me more intimately than any man could ever be. We remain husband and wife and, were I to remarry, this would not change.

Seek the acquaintance that is within and behind appearance, and no longer will you be bound to sorrow and suffering."

The Violent Man

Lady Mary was walking along in the woods one afternoon. A wicked man saw she was alone, and seeing her beauty, he lusted after her. So he set upon her, seeking to rape her. He pushed her to the ground and got on top of her. She did not scream or make any sound. She simply gazed into his eyes with the light of compassion, and she smiled. He became entranced by her gaze, and she said to him, "Here, my brother, I give you what you desire. Take it." But something shifted in him. The violence of lust departed from him, and he was shocked to see what he was doing. He began to cry and he got off of her. Mary laid hands on him and healed his spirit. He begged her forgiveness, and Mary forgave him and said, "My brother, you have my forgiveness, and I give you my peace, the peace of the Risen One." It is said that he was a very different man after that day and that he gave his life over to the service of others.

It was not uncommon for the Bride to heal the spirits of evil-doers and to bring about a radical change in their lives for the good. She had an innate knowing of the goodness in creatures and she had great skill in bringing it forth from within them. She understood perfectly the emptiness of darkness and all appearances.

The Bridal Chamber

Mary was giving teachings on the wedding feast, and the meaning of the bread and wine Melchizedek brought out. A disciple inquired of Mary, "Beloved, what is the nature of the bridal chamber?" Mary said, "It is the place where fire and light embrace and are joined. It is the place where the soul is gathered up and united with the Risen One. It is the Supernal Abode. Yet it is one's own heart, for there the Anointed is seated, as upon one's head. The Bridegroom is not 'Yeshua' and the Bride is not 'Mary.' The Bride and Bridegroom are the Spirit of the Messiah in you. The Lord is within us. The Spirit of the Lord is within and all around us. Here and now is the bridal chamber for those who are willing to intimate acquaintance."

Transference of the Soul

Lady Mary was giving secret instruction to a dear disciple on the methods of the transference of the soul between bodies. At one point, the soul of Mary entered into the body of her disciple and the disciple's soul entered into her body, so that they gazed at one another through each other's eyes. At first, the disciple became amazed, but then she became frightened and passed out. When she awoke she was in her own body again. Mary said to her, "My dear sweet child, do not be afraid. These bodies are as vessels into which the soul is poured. In much the same way you and I moved between bodies, so also can you move from the body of death to the body of life. You need only generate the Body of Light to acquire the Resurrection, and you need only transfer your soul into the Body of Light to enter the Ascension. What I have shown you is life. Do not fear death and dying. It is merely the passage into new life."

The Greater Healing

St. Mary Magdalene was speaking with some of her disciples when a companion arrived and said, "My Lady, your friend Anna is dying and sent me to ask you to come and save her." Lady Mary said to her disciples, "Let us go to our sister."

The woman was, indeed, on her deathbed when Mary and her companions arrived. The feeling of death loomed in the whole house. Mary entered, sat down at the side of Anna, and she took hold of her hand. Anna said to Mary, "I know you have the power to heal me, Blessed Lady. Please heal me. The angel of death is very near and I see his image moving among the shadows. He stalks my soul to take it from the world and I am afraid." Mary said to her, "I am willing that you are healed, my sister, and the Mother Spirit is willing, but it shall not come to pass in this old and worn-out body. It is time to remove this body like old and soiled clothing and to put on the body of the

Resurrection. Come now, I will lead you and you do not need to be afraid." Anna died that day; yet she was raised to life by the Holy Bride.

A disciple of Mary asked her, "I have seen you heal, my Lady, and I have seen you bring the dead back to life. Why did you not save your dear friend Anna?" Mary said, "The greater healing is not in the body. It is beyond the body. This day Anna was made whole and complete in the Risen Savior. She is saved for all time. What more than this could be done for a loved one?"

Restoration of the Well

Our Lady was out preaching in the land and she came to a village in distress because the well of the village had run dry. Now Mary was renowned for her wonders among the people, and when the people saw her enter the village, they believed God had sent them a savioress. They beseeched Our Lady's intervention. Mary agreed.

Mary chose twelve mothers and grandmothers of the village and gathered them about the well. Then Mary prayed to the Heavenly Father and Earthly Mother, she invoked the name of the Lord and the Mother Spirit, and together, she and the women sang heart songs at the well. By grace, the well was restored and made full. Mary said to the people, "Now let me give you living water from the well of Our Holy Mother, so that both your body and soul might not suffer thirst." The people received her and she taught them the Way.

Standing Stones

In the circle of Our Lady, many different sacred rites were taught. She taught the five holy rites of perfect gnosis, the rites of the holy grail and sacred lance, and the path of the sun and moon, among others. So, too, did she teach the Rite of the Standing Stone and the Great Circle. Every stone gathered for the ceremony was baptized and anointed. Once purified and consecrated, the stones were set into place. When everything was in place, the circle was sanctified with fire, and with praise and thanksgiving. The companions of the assembly would sing, dance, intone invocations, and worship in the presence of Yahweh. The standing stones pointed upward, in remembrance of Our Heavenly Father; the circle was consecrated in remembrance of Our Earthly Mother, and in that place heaven and earth were joined. It was a celebration of the Divine Life.

Mary taught individuals to perform the same sacred rite with five stones, one for each direction and one as the standing stone in the center. It was a way of blessing the people and the land and a way of mystical prayer. In each stone was a holy letter of the blessed name, and the light and fire of the Supernal Abode was brought down in that place. Thus she taught her disciples to make sacred places of prayer and meditation—this being but one of the ways.

The Witness of the Gospel in Nature

Mary led her companions in prayer and meditation at dawn. Afterward, she taught them, saying, "Just before dawn, when the bright morning star arises, it is like the Place of Truth, for as subtle and sublime as the light of predawn is the Body of Truth that leads to repose. Many ask, 'How shall we live and attain life?' Truly, I say, recognize the life that is in you, and the Light within the Light, going beyond glory into the essence of Light. So also I say to you, witness what creation and nature does, for therein is God's presence and wisdom disclosed. Look and see! At dawn, the birds of the air raise their voices in praise of their Creator. When the sun is setting, they do the same. No one need tell them anything, for in themselves they know what to do. In the same way, the Spirit and Truth are in you, and they are reflected in creation and nature all around you. Look and see, and you will know the Way, for the Gospel of Truth is written everywhere above and below, and it is engraved in your very own heart."

The Clumsy Woman

A woman came to Mary and said to her, "My Lady, I do not know what is wrong with me. I suffer ill fortune constantly and I am clumsy. I am always having accidents. Perhaps unclean or evil spirits plague me. I do not know. Please dear Lady, can you look and see the cause?"

Mary said, "There are wounds you must heal in your heart and soul. Because you are a woman, you do not feel worthy of God, but you must see that you have drunk a poisonous lie and you must expel the demon of the lie. I know that your husband left you for another woman, but he is not the value of your womanhood. On account of this, you have fallen into yourself. Now, you must call upon the Mother Spirit to pick you up and you must get up. There is male and female in you. Let these be joined. Receiving your healing, worship Holy Being as a holy woman and enter into the Light."

When Mary said this, she embraced the woman. The woman cried, not in sorrow but in joy and with a sense of relief. For she could feel the peace and the presence in Our Lady. Feeling this, she was healed in herself and was uplifted by the Holy Spirit. Mary said to her, "Come and stay with me. I will show you the good company of the Lord." And so the woman stayed in the company of Lady Mary and was among her companions from that day on. Mary gathered many broken women and made them whole.

The Angel of Death

Servants of a wealthy family came to Lady Mary and said, "The child of our house is gravely ill and near death. Please, Mistress, come and heal her." Mary said, "I will come." She took five of her disciples. They departed, and swiftly enough they were at the house. When they arrived, Mary put a disciple at each corner of the house, and she instructed them in a meditation. Then she put a disciple inside the house and gave her instructions as well. Once her disciples were set in place, Mary went into the little girl's room, and she herself stood guard by the girl's bed. Mary blessed the room and invoked the presence of the four great angels of the circle, and she set up wards of the Spirit against all unclean and dark spirits. Once she had done this, she renamed the child after her most beloved disciple, Salome.

In the midst of the ceremony, the angel of death drew near to the house but could not enter because of those who stood guard. Then Azrael summoned a demon to enter into the house and seek out the little girl, for it was the time of her death. The demon entered into the house but could not enter into the room because of the blessing Mary put upon it. Thus, the angel of death tried everything he could, but in vain. Unless he could draw very near and catch the girl's gaze, he could not take her soul from the world.

Now once the naming ceremony was complete, Mary healed the little girl and restored her to life. Then, she presented her to her family with her new name, and she was received as a new daughter. The father of the little girl gave thanks to Mary and he blessed God's name. He tried to give Mary a large sum of money, but Mary refused to take it. She said to the man, "This is blood money and the profits of oppression; the poor have died for you to gain it. This has brought ill fortune on your house and upon your family. If you wish to do something, then tend to justice and care for the poor, and seek to serve the God of Truth."

The Life of the Bride

Lord Yeshua walked in the world and taught the Way for several years, but Our Lady taught for many years, until at a ripe old age the end of her days came. Lady Mary performed countless wonders, and she taught all manner of secrets and mysteries. Her circle grew large and strong, so that many were well established in the Way by Our Lady. If we cannot write of all the wonders Our Lord performed or all of the holy teachings he imparted and yet he was among us so few years, how could we ever tell the tale of Our Lady in full? Truly, it is impossible. Yet anyone who desires can know her; she will reveal herself to all who call upon her. No one will be lacking in knowledge of her who seeks to know her, for she is ever near. Look and see!

The Death of St. Mary Magdalene

When Our Lady drew near unto death, she called her disciples to her. She spoke softly to them and blessed each and every one of them. To each she gave her heart advice, and then she said to them, "Now it is time for you to learn how to die and to depart from the fear of death once and for all." Our Lady said, "My Mother, into the grace of your womb I surrender my spirit." In this way, calmly and with grace, Our Lady shed the body.

When she had died, those who were present saw the radiant image of St. Mary of Magdal standing near her body smiling upon them. Then she departed from among them. It is said that a great luminous assembly appeared after her and that rainbows and light rays appeared in the skies. According to the tradition, she did not ascend, but honored her holy vow and went straight into another womb to be reborn again in a woman's form. So it is that she continues to come among us as a holy woman.

Many are the tales surrounding the death of the Holy Bride, but this is the essence of them all.

The New Holy Land

The Holy Mother departed this world by divine rapture, being taken up in ascension into heaven and leaving no body behind. Our Lady left her body behind so that it might be a seed of Light for a new holy land. Old Jerusalem was shortly to fall and the Promised Land had become profane. Therefore, it was good that a new land should be blessed and consecrated as a place of holy remembrance. Thus, among many Gnostics, old Jerusalem and what the outer and unspiritual church calls the "holy land" no longer has meaning. If the faithful and elect were to set out on holy pilgrimage, it would likely be to southern France to walk in the holy land of the Bride, Our Lady.

Yet, concerning the holy land and New Jerusalem, we must say this: Wherever the elect walk, that ground is holy and the kingdom of the Anointed is not of this world. The truth of Messianic consciousness is in the world of Supernal Light above, and it is within and all around us. New Jerusalem is the present truth of those who embody supernal or Messianic consciousness. This is what the Anointed Bride taught us, and it is what we have seen and heard in her. Praise the Living One, the Risen Savior, and praise Kallah Messiah who was and is to come!

Incarnations of the Holy Bride

The Lord ascended into the repose of the Living Father, but Our Lady continues to incarnate among us, moving in the Divine Mother as we also live, move, and have our being in her. From one generation to another, the soul of Our Lady is incarnate as a holy woman. From her holy soul are seven rays, so that, in truth, she appears as seven holy women, each embodying a face of the Holy Bride. From one, there are seven, and from seven there are seven times seven, so that a matrix of forty-nine is manifest in the world—such is the Divine Pleroma of the soul of the Bride. One is the secret center of the matrix of the Holy Bride, and seven are the inmost circle, and the rest radiate out in circles of seven. Thus, she comes as one and many; and her holy soul is always among us, laboring to give birth to the Second Coming of Christ. So it shall be until her labor comes to fruition.

The Second Coming: Reception of the Holy Bride

From one generation to another, the true apostolic succession continues, and there are adepts and masters, both men and women, who embody something of supernal or Messianic consciousness. Yet, until there is a greater realization of Messianic consciousness among human beings and a full reception of Christ as male and female, we await the Second Coming—for such is the true nature of the Second Coming. Today, there are relatively few who embody the Light-presence in full, but at the time of the Second Coming there shall be many. Today, few can receive Christ in female form; thus an imbalance remains in human consciousness. Therefore, according to the tradition, the Second Coming will not transpire through a holy man. Rather, it will occur through a holy woman. It is not the return of the soul of Yeshua but of the soul of St. Mary Magdalene, the Anointed Bride.

Some have said that a holy woman will appear and be recognized as the incarnation of Christos. Others have said that a holy woman will attain supernal consciousness, give birth to a daughter, and it will be her daughter who is the Christ-bearer. In modern times, prophets of the Bride's reception have seen a different vision: It is the vision of a matrix of the Christ-presence embodied by a number of holy women. Thus, seers in our age speak of the Second Coming as brought about by many holy women, not a single woman alone. Likewise, they speak of a wave of supernal or Messianic consciousness in women and men alike.

In any case, among Sophians, the Second Coming is the advent of the Mother Spirit and Holy Bride and is seen as something that will transpire through womanhood, just as the First Coming transpired through manhood and Christ was received as a holy man. Until a holy woman is received as the Christ-bearer in the same way Yeshua was received, the fullness of the Christ revelation is incomplete. Thus it is said, "Our Lord has come and Our Lady is coming!" And we pray, "May Our Lady come swiftly, may the Holy Bride be received among us!" Amen.

Notes

1. In Gnostic texts, "Agatho Daimon" is a name frequently used for the Great Spirit; it has also been called the "Living Father" and "Mother Spirit" among Gnostics.

2. Alternatively, a "Mage of Light."

3. Baptism, Anointing, and Eucharist; a common Gnostic initiation, but also an inward spiritual practice.

4. A name for the angel of death, hence "Brother Death."

5. These are three faces of Sophian Nigrans, or Dark Wisdom: "Mistress of the Night," "Queen of Demons," and the "Hag of Chaos," respectively.

6. Literally, "Dark Mother, Bright Mother."

7. In legend, this is said to be a rite by which dark spirits are oath-bound to serve as "wrathful guardians" of the Light-transmission.

8. "Divine Fullness."

9. Literally, "correction," "mending," or "healing," and indicates the specific work each soul must accomplish in the process of self-realization.

CYCLE 6

THE SECRET GOSPEL OF
ST. MARY MAGDALENE

THE SECRET GOSPEL OF ST. MARY MAGDALENE

1 These are sayings spoken by Salome the maiden in the name of St. Mary Magdalene, which women of wisdom have held in trust. Mary said, "If you know the Woman of Light, you will know your Mother and be reborn of the Mother Spirit as a child of Light. Because the Light is bornless, you will have eternal life."

2 Mary was speaking to her companions, and she said, "There is glory of glory, and glory of light, and there is the True Light. Seek, therefore, the essence of the Light, which is beyond all, and you shall know the Truth of Light."

3 Mary said, "This world is a cemetery. It is filled with corpses. For this reason, the Lord set the world on fire so that the dead might awaken and spirits might be set free. And now the fire burns, and we tend it so that it might burn brightly, and we dance within the fire, for we are on fire with the Spirit of Yahweh. If you seek the Anointed, you seek the fire, and when you are utterly burnt away, you will rejoice in the True Light."

4 A woman asked Mary, "Are you the one the Lord loved dearly?" Mary said, "The Lord loved the world, and he gave Light and life to the world, so that no longer would anyone have to live in darkness. He loved me as the Soul of the World, so that embracing me he might embrace the world and uplift it to the bridal chamber. I am she whom the Lord loves, as is the soul of Light in you." Mary said, "The one who finds me will find the Anointed, for I am the house in which the Lord dwells."

5   The companions said to Mary, "Tell us about New Jerusalem."
    Mary said, "It is Wisdom, not of this world, but of the World
    of Supernal Light. When all of the sparks are gathered in and
    all of the vessels of light are mended, you will see the glory of
    New Jerusalem coming out of heaven, and in it you will be-
    hold the bridal chamber and the image of the Anointed One
    in it."

6   Mary said, "What is cast down shall be lifted up, and what is
    lifted up shall be thrown down; what is on high must be
    brought down upon the earth, and the earth must be lifted on
    high."

7   Mary said, "Fire is above water, and the sky is above the earth.
    All of these are above and below, and all are joined in the
    Mother's womb, which is the primordial space from which they
    all arise. Everything will return to its root and essence."

8   Mary said to a woman, "The Mother is everything, and she is
    nothing. She is everything here below, and she is nothing in
    the embrace of the Father above. Yet above and below she is
    the same, and here she is always changing. You are she and
    she is you."

9   Mary once said, "Do not concern yourself with the darkness in
    the world, but banish the darkness that is in you. Because it
    will bind you and destroy you if you do not cast it out of you."

10 Mary said, "Give what you wish to receive and you shall have
    it. Take what you desire and it will be stolen from you."

11 Mary said to her disciples, "Eve and Lilith are one woman, and
    she is a supernal emanation. If a woman knows herself she will
    know the Holy Woman, just as if a man knows himself he will
    know the Supernal Adam. To acquire this knowledge you must
    be single, which is to say undivided."

12 Disciples of Mary said to her, "We are going on a pilgrimage
    to the holy land so we might see where you and the Lord
    lived." Mary said to them, "The holy land is wherever a child

of Light goes, and it is where the child of Light abides. The holy land is where the Anointed and the soul are joined. It is the bridal chamber."

13 Mary said, "When you also pay the ransom, then you will be ransomed, and no longer will you be held hostage."

14 Mary said, "Christ has one Mother, and she is the Queen of Heaven. The body is born of the Earthly Mother, but the soul of Light is born of the Heavenly Mother, and it is the Mother Spirit that awakens the soul of Light. Mary gave birth to a child in the world, but the Mother Spirit gave birth to Christ. So it is with all who are anointed with Supernal Light."

15 Mary said to Salome, "We are dead because the Lord died, and we are alive because the Lord lives. The tomb is the Mother's womb to those who are among the living."

16 Mary said to some women, "If you know the path of the moon, you will know the path of the sun. With this knowledge and understanding, follow the path of Light, which is beyond the sun or the moon. This is the path of the cross."

17 Mary said to her disciples, "The cross is the limit, for it binds the power of the demiurgos and Satan, which is death. Death has never existed. The Lord has shown us this and now we must remember."

18 Mary once said, "A woman who knows how to bake bread understands the purpose of yeast, and she includes yeast in the dough, though only a little bit. So has the Mother put the fiery intelligence in human beings, knowing they will ascend because of it."

19 Mary said, "Until there is Light in a form and it becomes Light, it is a false appearance. Though a human form appears, unless a person brings the Supernal Soul into the body, that person is not yet a human being."

20 A woman said to Mary, "You saw the Risen Savior first. What did he look like?" Mary said to her, "He looked like no man nor angel nor god, but his appearance was the image of the

Human One, the image and likeness of the Living God. Truly I tell you, whoever beholds the Risen Savior, it is as though he or she is the first to see him."

21 Mary said, "Everyone knows how to clean a house, but few know how to make themselves clean inwardly. If you know how to clean a house but do not know how to clean yourself inwardly, then your house and all that you touch are unclean. Nothing is unclean to a person who is clean. This is what the Lord taught his disciples."

22 Mary taught, "If you are violent, then your end will be violent, but if you acquire the peace of the Lord, then you will end in peace."

23 Mary spoke, and said, "There is baptism, chrism, and wedding feast, and there is the ransom and bridal chamber. Baptism is water, chrism is fire, and the ransom is earth. The wedding feast is the air, for in the Spirit we shall meet the Anointed in the air on the Day of Joy, and then the element of the bridal chamber shall be fully revealed. Everything the Lord accomplished he accomplished in a mystery, and the Anointed Bride is the mystery."

24 Mary said, "Ask the Mother Spirit and she will show you the face of our Father. When you look and see it, you will meet the gaze of the Beloved, for he is the image of the Living Father."

25 Mary said, "Know how to love and you will be undivided. This is the repentance the Lord taught, and it is the perfect baptism."

26 A woman said to Mary, "You are the holiness of womanhood we have been waiting to see." Mary said to her, "What have you been doing while you were waiting? If you see this in me, then it is in you. All the while it has been with you! What were you waiting for?"

27 A young lady said to Mary, "When will the world be transformed?" Mary said, "It will not be transformed, but it is sacred to the Mother already. When you are transformed the world

will be transformed, for you are the world and the world is you. The world is changing all of the time, and yet it is unchanged. The Mother is changing continually, yet she is ever the same, yesterday, today and tomorrow. Become as the Mother and you will see the Great Transformation, yet nothing will have changed."

28 Mary said, "When the Lord died the world passed away, and when the Lord was raised up a new creation came into being. When the pure emanation comes into the world it is the union of the beginning and the end, and all things are restored anew."

29 Someone asked to see the holy wounds on Mary and she said, "Here, look and see, but look also to see the Risen One; for unless you see among the living, all that you see are dead things."

30 A woman said to Mary, "Our Lady, you are a great prophetess. Praise the Lord who sent you among us." Mary said, "You also must be a seer, for one who sees lives."

31 Salome reclined with Mary at the table, and Salome said to Mary, "You, Bride of Light, are most blessed of women, for you have known the Lord most intimately and have become fire and light." Mary said to her, "Because you know the truth, you also are light and fire and Spirit. In the whole of creation there is nothing else, only light and fire and Spirit."

32 Mary said, "There are seven heavens, seven earths, and seven hells, and there are worlds within worlds, and realms within realms. All shall pass away, but the Supernal Abode shall abide eternal. There is no end to God's Word or Wisdom."

33 Mary said, "Know how to cleave, and the husks shall be shed, and you will be joined to the Living One. The perfection of cleaving is the bridal chamber and the wedding feast is the glory of that perfect aeon."

34 Mary said, "No one finds the Lord save those to whom the Lord reveals himself, for the Lord seeks his own and has come for the elect."

35 Mary said to some people, "If you are seeking, it is the Holy Spirit that is seeking in you, and so be assured you will find. Recognizing this, you have found already, and what you have found is life."

36 Mary said, "One who clings to the world, clings to a corpse, and one who clings to a corpse is unclean. There is a rite of purification for one who becomes unclean by touching a corpse, but first one must let go of the corpse and seek life."

37 Mary said, "The Divine Mother is Light and she is darkness, she is the saint and she is the sinner, angels and demons are images in her, as are the gods and all of the archons; yet she is beyond all of these. Know her in all things and you will be free of bondage, even as the Anointed is free."

38 A woman said to Mary, "I have seen the light!" Mary said to the woman, "Wonderful! Now join the darkness to it, and go into the light, and you will discover what is beyond appearances."

39 Mary once said, "Deeply my body mourned for the Lord, but deeper still my soul within me rejoiced. Do not cling to the image on the cross, but cleave to the image of the Risen Savior."

40 Mary said, "A tree has life in it because of the sap, and we have life in us because of the chrism. Unless one has the chrism, one is not Christian but steals the name. Be certain you do not steal."

41 Mary said, "I was with the Risen Savior, and beheld the Mother. In the first heaven, she was the Radiant Earth of Paradise. In the second heaven, she was the Starry Night Sky. In the third heaven, she was a Great Fire. In the fourth heaven, she was the Great Angel and Celestial Temple, and the Holy Sacrifice. When I beheld her in the fifth heaven, she was the Glory of the Anointed abiding there, and in the sixth heaven, she was Fire and Ice and the End-of-Days. In the seventh heaven, she was the Great Luminous Assembly, and the Holy Throne, and the image of the One-Who-Sits-Upon-the-

Throne; but in the Supernal Abode I cannot say what she was like. One must go look and see for oneself."

42 Mary said, "When the Anointed descended into Hades and the realms of Gehenna, the chosen came to him, drawn to the Light, but many spirits fled from him, unwilling to enter into the Light. It was the same when he walked upon the earth; the insider drew near but the outsiders were driven away."

43 Mary said to her disciples, "When the Risen Savior appears, look into his heart, and there you will see a threefold flame of Sophia. It is faith, hope, and love, but inwardly it is knowledge, understanding, and wisdom. Ask the Lord to give you this holy flame, so that you also might enter the kingdom and be perfect as the Father and Son are perfect."

44 Mary to her companions, "There is power in the blood of Christ and glory in the body of Christ, the essence and presence of the Supernal Emanations. When you eat of the wedding feast, bind your soul to the Light-emanations. Ascending, you will descend with Light, and descending you will ascend with the Truth."

45 Mary said, "You go down into the water and you die, because the reflection is shattered on the surface. When you rise up you come alive, for knowing your origin you no longer cling to a reflection or an image, but are reborn of your true essence. The nature of this essence is no-thing, and knowing this you will rule over the entirety."

46 Mary said, "The Lord said, 'Do not make a home for yourselves in the world, but be at home in the Spirit.'"

47 Mary said, "Many are the apostles the Lord has sent, and they are rays of light flowing out of the Spiritual Sun. Many are the apostles the Bride shall send, and they are flames of fire leaping out of her. If you receive one whom the Bridegroom and Bride sends, then you receive one who comes from the Pleroma of Light. Woe to them who reject the apostles of Light, for they have rejected their own soul! Receive every person who

comes to you walking in holiness and beauty, for they are your fathers and mothers, your brothers and sisters, and your little ones."

48 Mary taught her disciples, saying, "The Aeons of Light are the handmaids of the Bride at the wedding feast, and the best man is the son of Adam at the wedding; in the bridal chamber the soul acquires intimate acquaintance with the Anointed and becomes the Anointed. Until that time, sing and dance and rejoice, for it is to those who abide in joy that the Shekinah comes, and it is through her that you will enter the bridal chamber."

49 Mary said, "Come, let us go in. The Lord is waiting. If the mark is in you, then it is a sin to go outside. The righteous are those who live inwardly in the presence of the Anointed."

50 Mary said, "A man once came to the Lord seeking an answer, but the Lord sat in silence. When the man departed, the Lord said, 'Perhaps he was not seeking, but if he was, then surely he has his answer.' Many times the Lord said nothing, but an answer was given. Remember this when you pray, for the power of prayer is silence."

51 Mary said, "What is a woman to do against a strong man? She cannot overcome him. When faced with a strong man, if she cannot call out to a righteous man for help, then her only choice is not to resist him. Now I ask you, is this right? Indeed! For she will live and the day of justice will come! Yet it is wrong, for this demonstrates the dominion of falsehood in this world. There is great power in womanhood but it is hidden, and many men and beasts of the field seem to have power, but inwardly are weak. In the World of Supernal Light, only the soul that has power in it will have power, and those lacking the power of Truth will not appear in it. This world is a world of falsehood, but the world-to-come is a World of Truth. Do not be deceived by appearances and do not doubt there will be justice!"

52 Mary taught, "Once you come to the light and know the light is in you, you cannot continue to walk in the ways of darkness, lest you will fall into a greater darkness. No! You must walk in the Light and enter the Light, and bring forth the Light from within you, for only then will you be established in the Way of Life."

53 Mary said to her disciples, "Do not receive every spirit that comes to you, but put every spirit to the test to see if it comes from God or the demiurge or Satan. There are many false lights, and they glitter and glow, and even a demon can appear in the image of the Risen One. Do not be deceived, but look always for the light of Love and Truth, for what is evil lacks Love and what is mixture lacks the perfection of Truth. In the Holy Spirit you will be empowered to discern, for she is discerning awareness."

54 Mary said, "The Lord laid down a ransom for your soul, yet if you do not receive the Spirit of the Lord and live as a free person, then the ransom does not take effect. Only a free person can gather and give ransom, and so set free a hostage. Everything you see the Lord do, you must also do. This is the Way of Freedom."

55 The disciples of Mary said, "Tell us about Grandmother Israel?" Mary said to them, "She has seen the End-of-Days and the Beginning-of-Life, and she is ancient, yet she is ever young. She is the understanding of wisdom, and knowledge of truth, the perfection of awareness. All is in her sight, yet she desires nothing. She is the fruition of womanhood having given birth to Divine illumination."

56 Mary said, "Until you know the darkness of Sophia, you will not acquire her Light. Unless you die and are reborn of the Mother Spirit, the knowledge of the Resurrection will elude you."

57 Mary said, "Do not think the cross is wood, for it is light. Do not think the Anointed is a man, for he is an emanation. Do not become bound by appearances, for the Spirit of Truth is invisible. Do not be idolaters."

58 Mary said, "Pray that you have an eye that sees, an ear that hears, a tongue that tastes, a nose that smells, and a body that feels. For many are they who are dead, whose senses perceive nothing, but you have been called to life and raised from the dead. Therefore, pray to be fully alive."

59 Mary said, "There are many gods and goddesses with great power, and all manner of spirits that have secret knowledge, yet the power that is in you is greater and the knowledge you possess is more rare and precious. I tell you, great and luminous beings shall come seeking power and knowledge from you. See that you give to all who ask and withhold only from those who come to steal, and those who receive let worship the Anointed of God Most High."

60 Mary said, "I tell you truly, you are Divine beings, but do not let anyone worship you."

61 Once Mary said, "In the Anointed you are free from bondage to the law and the dominion of the archons. Do not make yourself a slave again, but live as a free man or woman in the Holy Spirit."

62 Mary said to her disciples, "Unless you go out of your homeland and follow the Spirit through the wilderness into the Promised Land as I have, you cannot be a disciple to me. Unless you bear the marks of the crucifixion that I bear, you cannot be a disciple to the Lord. When you receive the call, you must go forth and not look back, for the one who looks back shall be bound, but the one who looks to the Anointed will be set free."

63 Mary was teaching one day, and she said, "The warden and guards will pursue anyone attempting to escape from prison, and dark spirits will arise to oppose anyone who shines with Light. Do not fear the persecution you face on account of the Risen Savior and Mother Spirit, but have faith and endure, for your freedom is already won and all darkness has come to an end."

64 Mary said, "If you desire something, ask the Mother, for she gives to her children all that they desire."

65 Mary's disciples asked her, "How should we worship God?" Mary said, "With tears and with laughter, and in all that you do, and with song and dance, and in every way the Spirit inspires. Worship in the Spirit of Truth, with your heart and your soul, your mind and your body; live in the presence of Yahweh always."

66 Mary said, "Do not mistake the rites performed outwardly for the true sacred rite, for unless the sacred rites transpire inwardly, the outward rites are only husks of darkness."

67 Mary said, "Receiving the baptism of water, seek also the baptism of fire and the Spirit, for only when you are baptized with fire and the Spirit is your baptism complete."

68 Mary said, "The Anointed has sown seeds of Light, and you are the secret garden of the Anointed, and in due season the harvest shall come. Tend to your growth now so that you might be ripe and mature when the harvest comes."

69 Mary said, "The mystery of the bridal chamber is private; it can only be spoken in the presence of one, and only if it is known to that one already. Do not speak in public about things that are private, but be wise in your speech."

70 Mary taught, "Many have followed their heart, and it led them astray. Yet, it was not their heart that they followed but some other spirit. The Lord is seated there, in your heart, and you must know your heart to know the Lord. There is a husk of darkness surrounding the heart. When that husk is broken and falls away, then you will know your heart and know the Lord. Let your heart be circumcised so that you might enter into the fullness of love and be intimately acquainted."

71 Mary said, "To gain recognition is to become what you see, for no one sees anything he or she has not become. If a person is not able to recognize the Anointed, or one whom the Anointed sends, it is because the Anointed does not indwell that person. Therefore, when there is recognition rejoice, for your salvation is near and you have entered the kingdom."

72 Mary said, "Unless you know the kingdom in you, you will not see it outside of you; unless the Anointed indwells you, you will not find the Anointed in the world."

73 Mary said, "We are Christian until we become Christ, and the Lord has promised every true Christian will become Christ. This is our spiritual hope."

74 The disciples inquired of Mary about the World of Supernal Light. She said to them, "It is above and below, within you and beyond you, and all around you, but few are they who have eyes to see it, and fewer still who dwell in it."

75 A disciple asked Mary, "When will the Second Coming occur?" Mary said, "It can happen at any time, anywhere, when you least expect it. It is the mystery of the Perfect Aeon known only to the Living Father, which he will reveal in the Mother in due season. Therefore, be ready and live without regrets, so that when it transpires you will be among the living."

76 Mary said, "Only one who is passionate for truth will discover the truth."

77 A man asked Mary, "Who is greater, you or Yeshua?" Mary said to him, "Truly I tell you, the Anointed is the Anointed, whether male or female, and the Anointed is exalted above every head, even the highest among the angels in heaven and Aeons of Light. As for Yeshua, he is greater than I, for I received everything from him. So it is for every disciple, he or she is never greater than the teacher."

78 Mary was teaching in the assembly, and a woman exclaimed, "Now is the hour of the Holy Bride!" Mary said, "No, before the Bride is received, she must be rejected, and before the Second

Coming there must come a great darkness. Until the Second Coming of Christ, the Wisdom of God shall not be received. When the Bride is received, know the Second Coming is near."

79   Mary said, "If you know what the world is, you will no longer desire it, for you will see what is beyond the world. When you see what is beyond the world, in that day it will be in the world."

80   A young disciple asked Mary, "How can I come to know the Lord?" Mary said, "Become empty, like a cup, and let the Mother Spirit pour the Lord and her presence into you."

81   Mary said, "Seek to commune with the angels of our Heavenly Father and the angels of our Earthly Mother, and cleaving to the Lord in your heart, let the heavens and earth be joined."

82   Mary said, "All things exist in and with one another, and while they exist they depend on one another, but when the time of dissolution comes, all things will return to their own root and essence. What has come from above returns to the abode from which it has come, and what comes from below returns to its origin. What is in between has never existed, and will return to the great void."

83   Mary said, "Is it not written, 'In the beginning was void and chaos?' Yet, did not God exist before the beginning? If order and light came into being, surely these are of God. As for the void and chaos, these are the primordial ground from which God has created; and the one creating is the demiurge. For in truth, what God creates is emanation, and the emanations of God create. Therefore, Yahweh emanated and Elohim created. There is no beginning to this, nor is there an end. Consider this when you meditate on the End-of-Days."

84   Mary said, "Did God give birth to creation without a womb? No, indeed! For creation is in God's womb, and until it is complete it shall not emerge."

85   Mary said, "When the soul departs this world it must travel through many realms in between, and it must pass through the realms of the archons, and the heavens, and the great abyss. Powers will arise to prevent the soul's ascent, and guardians will seek to bind it to their realms. Yet those who cleave to the Anointed, in whom the Holy Spirit dwells, they will be invisible to the powers and guardians. Already, they are free!"

86   Mary said, "From the purity of space, air arose; from air, fire arose; from fire, water; and from these, the earth came into being. When you depart the world, let the elements dissolve into one another, and let the mother and father essences be joined; then wait upon the Spirit of the Lord, abiding in the Transparent Light of the Supernal Abode. In this way, you will attain repose."

87   A woman said to Mary, "I am dying and wish to go to God. What should I do?" Mary said, "Gather yourself as a sun in your heart, and envision the Risen Savior come for you. When the Savior appears, as light, rise up to meet him in the air and the Anointed will receive you in God."

88   Mary said, "Labor while you are in the field, and rest when you are called home. Do not be idle while you live, lest you depart the world in poverty."

89   Mary said, "Because of the power of the demiurgos, you have forgotten yourself. You believe you are a child of darkness, yet you are a child of Light. Indeed! Truly, I say to you, you are a person of Light who has come from the Light, and if you remember yourself, you will know where your home is. This is the remembrance of the wedding feast, regarding which the Lord instructed us, 'Do this in remembrance of me.'"

90   Mary said, "What the Anointed is, I am and you are, for this reason the Anointed has come, to remind those caught in the spell of forgetfulness."

91   Mary said, "Beware! If you blaspheme the Mother Spirit, there will be no one to save you, for she is the Spirit of salvation and your very life."

92 Mary said, "Weave for yourselves garments of light, so that, when you go before the Queen of Heaven to be received, you do not appear naked. With faith and the fullness of knowledge, do good works and love one another, and in the Spirit of the Lord you will have garments of light."

93 Mary once said, "Blessed is one who knows sorrow and suffering, for that person will know life."

94 Mary said, "You cannot destroy the evil inclination, but if you bring it into the service of the good, it will no longer be evil."

95 Mary said, "When the saint receives the Anointed it is good, but when the sinner receives the Anointed it is better, for entering into the light the sinner is more powerful than the saint."

96 Mary said to her disciples, "You are midwives of the Mother Spirit, and you are meant to labor with her in the harvest of souls. Yet do not grasp on to the fruit of your labors, for it is she who accomplishes everything and to whom all good fruits belong."

97 Mary said, "No one will know the Living Father apart from the Mother, for it is she who shows us the face of our Father."

98 Mary spoke, and she said, "Having awakened, remain awake, and keep vigil, ever waiting upon the Lord."

99 Mary said to her companions, "Preach the Gospel to all good creatures, and bear forth the light into all realms. If the wind will listen, teach the wind. If a ghost seeks redemption, then bless the ghost. Speak the truth to all spirits and creatures, for in the Human One all are blessed and all are received."

100 Mary said, "Know when to retreat and when to live. When you retreat, be silent and die to yourself, so that you might be alive in the Spirit. When you live, be alive and vibrant, and rejoice each day in the presence of God."

101 Mary said to her disciples, "The Human One is the divinity of the holy Shabbat, and the Shekinah is the companion of all

who remember and keep it. The Lord has ordained the Shabbat as a blessing for all who desire to draw near. It is a great blessing."

102 Mary said, "The Anointed is the Lord of the Shabbat, and it is the day of the Beloved. In it is the mystery of the bridal chamber, and those who honor it shall gain knowledge of the mystery."

103 Mary said, "In heaven, men and women who have love and knowledge of God are fully received in the light, but below only men of God are fully received, for this is an abode of falsehood and darkness, and the archons favor the male. Yet, the image of the Human One in the bridal chamber is male and female joined together in one body of light, like unto the holy angels. When the image below is as the image above, then the Gospel will be fulfilled."

104 Mary said to her disciples, "All aeons are not divine, but many are brought in by the demiurgos and archons and bear the taint of falsehood. The aeons are thoughts in the perfect intelligence of God, fashioned by Wisdom and Understanding. Yet under the influence of the demiurge, they are corrupted. Only the pure emanation of the Aeon of Light is free of taint or corruption, for it is the body of the Risen Savior whom the archons could not hold in bondage. And it shall come to pass that a false aeon shall replace the Aeon of Truth, for already the image in the bridal chamber is partial in the minds of men."

105 Mary said, "The Perfect Aeon is called Eternal Shabbat, and the soul of the Perfect Aeon is called the Christ, and it is Light and Truth. The seed of the Perfect Aeon has been sown in the world, in the human mind and heart, and it shall bear good fruit in due season. Until that time there are many aeons in conflict below the great abyss, and the world is a play of shadows and shades and dim glows. Therefore, do not be deceived, but cleave to the True Light, and pray for the Aeon of the

Holy Spirit in which all aeons will be rectified and the revelation of the Perfect Aeon complete."

106 Mary said, "The Anointed was joined by the Living Father to the Light-emanations, so that, when he appeared to us, their radiant holy breath and power was in him. This is the power of the Holy Spirit that he breathed upon us, akin to the Spirit of God moving upon the surface of the deep in the beginning. Yet, this Spirit that the Anointed breathed on us moved on the surface and the deep. On account of this breath of the Savior, a new creation has come into being, which is the purity of emanation."

107 Mary said to her companions, "There is light and fire in your breath. If you cleave to the Risen Savior and breathe as the Savior breathes, you will discover it. When you discover it, your whole body will become filled with fire and light and you will be transformed into the image of the Living One."

108 Mary said, "The aeons are perfect and eternal above, but their images below are inherently flawed. Seek to look and see them above so that you might join soul and image and rectify them."

109 Mary spoke these words in private. She said, "The body and blood of the Lord is fire and light, and the power of the Mother Spirit is in it. There is fire in the bread and light in the wine, and the Holy Spirit passes in between them and joins them. So are the Bride and Bridegroom joined, and it is for this reason it is called a wedding feast. Understand, the body and blood are not the image on the cross. They are the image of the Risen Savior, so that, consecrated, the power of the Risen Savior is in the bread and wine. What is the image of the Risen Savior? It is the image of the Groom and Bride united, called the Second Adam. This is the image of the Great Seth."

110 Mary said to her disciples, "Kali Kallah appears black to those who do not know her, yet to those who love her and who draw near, she is white brilliance. Her image is as the starry night sky, and the light of the heavens and Supernal Abode are in her. To pass beyond, you must enter her embrace, even as the Lord embraced her. Then, through Daughter Sophia you will acquire knowledge of Mother Sophia, the Queen of Heaven."

111 Mary said, "There is wisdom and there is wisdom, and the wisdom of the world is not the Wisdom of God. Seek, therefore, the truth of wisdom, that knowing the Wisdom of God, all wisdom might be redeemed in you."

112 Mary said, "The Logos emanated into the world for the redemption of Sophia. If the redemption of Sophia is not received in the world, then the world is not redeemed. Sophia received the Logos, and those who cleave to Sophia have received the Logos and they are redeemed. It is Sophia in you that receives the Logos and is saved."

113 Mary was speaking to her companions. She said, "Everything that is above is in you here below. The Light of the heavens and Supernal Abode is in you, and is the essence of the Perfect Aeon. Let Logos and Sophia embrace in you and you will behold great wonders. Nothing will be impossible to you, for what is above will be brought down below and what is below will be lifted above. Praise the Lord!"

114 Mary said, "Logos in the name of the Lord and Sophia is the name of the Bride. In the bridal chamber, their name is Christos."

115 Mary said to her disciples, "You have heard of the ascension of Enoch. When he ascended, he became male and female. The male entered into repose and the female moved to run and return; thus Metatron appeared in the height and Sandalphon in the depths. This is the great angel of the Lord, male and female, the image of Bride and Bridegroom. And it is the Supernal Image of our perfection."

116 Mary said, "God the Father entered in through the image of the Son, but the world was overwhelmed by the great supernal glory. Therefore, the Son imparted the Mother Spirit and God the Mother has entered in through the image of the Daughter to nurture the little ones until they grow wise. The light entered but was too bright, and so now the fire comes to purify so that all might be sanctified to receive the True Light. Everything shall be accomplished in due season, and it is the Mother Spirit that will accomplish everything."

117 Mary said, "We have Father and we have Mother, for God is our Father and our Mother, though, indeed, the Most High is beyond Father or Mother. There is no knowledge of the Father apart from the Mother, for it is Mother Spirit who gives birth to the image of the Son in whom the Living Father is revealed. So also shall Mother Spirit give birth to the image of the Daughter, so that the image of the Son will be perfect and the revelation of God Most High made complete. Truly I say to you, there is a holier Gospel yet to be spoken."

118 Mary said, "Under the law and old covenant, the circumcision applied only to men, but in the new covenant, women are also circumcised. Likewise, under the old covenant, only men were called as priests, but under the new covenant, women are also called as priestesses. The old covenant fell to the dominion of the demiurgos. It remains to be seen whether the new covenant shall stand or fall. If it falls, then another shall arise. Therefore, labor always for the perfection of the covenant, so that you are awake when the Aeon of the Holy Spirit enters in."

119 A woman said to Mary, "I have heard that the Lord walked on water." Mary said, "Indeed! The Lord did walk on water, and he walked on the firmaments of the heavens when he ascended to the Supernal Abode. Tell me, which is the greater wonder?"

120 Mary said to her disciples, "I was water, but the Lord made me wine. Now I may bring passion and joy to the hearts of human ones and a force of fire against the Great Beast."

121 Mary said, "In the Lord, men have an image of their perfection; in the Bride, women have an image of their perfection;

and it is a single perfection. Unless there is perfection in man and woman, the perfection of the Human One is incomplete. And so the Lord said to us, 'Be perfect as your Father in heaven is perfect.' For truly, the Father is not the Father, and the Mother is not the Mother, for the image of the Human One, which is the likeness and image of the Most High, is male and female joined together—the androgynous and self-begetting One. This is the truth of the Anointed."

122   Mary said, "Three days passed from the crucifixion to the resurrection, and so shall three days pass from the resurrection to the Second Coming. Let those who have ears listen and hear what the Spirit is speaking!"

123   Mary said, "If Christos can appear as a male, then surely Christos can appear as a female. Those who deny holiness in womanhood do not understand holiness in manhood or womanhood but are sorely bound to ignorance. Do not believe the father of lies. Believe in the Mother Spirit, whose name is the Spirit of Truth and Comforter!"

124   Mary said, "The beast of the field receives by grace, and the faithful receive by faith and grace; but it is the elect who receive by faith and knowledge and grace and, for this reason, are called 'the perfect.'"

125   Mary said, "Where darkness abides, the light cannot enter. When the light enters, all darkness vanishes. To enter into the light, you must banish the darkness that is in you, and when you enter the light, you must join the light and darkness to gain the acquaintance of the True Light. Unless you first let go of the darkness and cleave to the light, the light cannot enter, but once the light enters, all darkness shall be transformed and you will know the Truth beyond light or darkness. This is the Truth that will set you free!"

126   Mary said to her companions, "I tell you, there is a superior intelligence that shall come to those who wait upon the Spirit of the Lord. It is like thunder and lightning, and it will illuminate you."

127 Mary said, "If you seek knowledge of the Risen Savior, open yourself to the light that comes from above. It will awaken a fire in you and bring you into the fullness of knowledge, understanding, and wisdom, and you will lack nothing."

128 Mary said, "Where there is peace, God's Spirit abides. Therefore, make peace and you will know great joy."

129 Mary said, "If you cannot love, you cannot be united. One who is divided is destined for destruction. Therefore, the Savior taught us to love so that we might have life."

130 A woman said to Mary, "It is not my destiny to attain salvation, for it is not in the stars for me. The stars of my birth are ill-fated." Mary said, "It is not the stars that determine your fate, my sister. It is the Mother Spirit. According to the stars of her birth, Sarah was not destined to have a son, yet the Mother Spirit blessed Sarah and she had Isaac. If you have faith and seek true knowledge, you will not be bound by the fates that sin and the archons dictate, for in the Risen Savior your soul is exalted beyond the domains of the archons and the celestial regions. Believe in God, not in the abodes of the archons, and the Mother Spirit will fulfill your heart's desire. Your destiny is with Christ in God."

131 Mary said, "When you pray, join yourself to the Anointed by the power of the name, and cleave to the Light-emanations. Let your heart pray and use few words, and learn the delight of the prayer of silence. For it is in silence you will hear the Spirit of Yahweh speaking. This is how the Savior taught us to pray."

132 Mary said, "It is with passion that one must cleave, and all passions must be cleaving. Then you will experience the perfection of cleaving which is divine rapture."

133 Mary said, "When you have one thought and one desire, in that instant you will be fulfilled."

134 Mary said, "Abide where you are; there the Anointed is."

135 Mary said to her companions, "If you do not know your heart, you cannot know the Lord. For there, in your heart, is the indwelling Christ, and your inmost heart's desire is Christ. Therefore, knowing your heart you will know Christ, and in Christ, all your desires will be fulfilled."

136 Mary said, "Knowledge, understanding, and wisdom are not superior to love, for these come from union and it is love that unites. One who has love will have knowledge, understanding, and wisdom, but without love, no one is wise. If there is power without love, it is evil and will give birth to evil, but where there is love, power is exercised in wisdom. All good things come by way of love."

137 Mary said to her disciples, "If you desire to be free, set others free. Be forgiving and you will be forgiven."

138 Mary said to her disciples, "Of all things I wish you to have the Sacred Heart of Christ, which is compassion. For compassion is the womb of the Mother in which Christ is born, and in this, Christ will be born in you. Pray to the Mother Spirit to have her womb and to conceive and birth the Anointed in you. I will pray for you also."

139 Mary said, "Do not think the kingdom of the Anointed is of this world. It is not of this world. Yet do not think that you must depart this world to enter into the kingdom, for it has come near unto you this day and it is in you."

140 Mary said to her companions, "The Lord ascended to repose in the Father, but the Holy Bride remains with you. Invite her and welcome her. She will come to you and reveal herself to you. In her shall all mysteries of the Anointed be revealed and in her you will know the perfection of the Mother Spirit. You need only open your mind and heart and life to her; she will come and enter, and the Spirit of the Anointed will come with her. She will bring you into the bridal chamber."

141 Mary said, "If anything is written apart from the Spirit, it is dead, but if something is written and the Spirit is in you, it will be black fire on white fire that you will see, and there will be neither black nor white."

142 Mary said, "The Lord spoke with authority because the Living Father granted it to him and the Mother Spirit spoke in him. He was the presence and power of which he was speaking. You also seek this divine authority, so that you might also speak Truth."

143 Mary said, "There is no place among us for the undecided, for they have not yet received the call."

144 Mary said to her disciples, "The Lord has said that the Holy Spirit will reveal what has not been revealed, and that she will lead us into All-Truth. When her hour comes, this will come to pass, even as the Lord spoke it. Already it is coming to pass, though when she will move freely, no one knows."

145 Mary said, "If God were not alien, there would be no need for the divine revelation, for God would be known among humankind. Because, as yet, God is alien, revealers come and the revelation is ongoing."

146 Mary said, "You say I am a woman, but see, I am a man, and I am a woman, and I am neither man nor woman. You go looking for the Anointed, but do not see. So long as you are looking, you will not see. When your seeking comes to an end, you will find."

147 Mary said, "Pray with your heart, not your head, for your head will lead you astray."

148 Mary said to her companions, "Here you are, and here I am, and here the Lord is also."

149 Mary said, "I looked into the eyes of the Anointed and found no beginning, and so also I found no end. Everything is in the Anointed, the Father, the Mother, and the entirety; therefore, the whole is crucified and raised up with him. Yet, unless one acquires the knowledge of this, it has not transpired."

150 Mary spoke, and she said, "Do you not know that the True Light has been here from the very beginning, only it was not

activated? Now that it is activated, greater wonders than you have seen shall come to pass, and you will be among the wonders."

151 Mary said, "Pray the Holy Spirit moves so that you might recognize her, for then she can lead you into perfect repose, even as she led the Son to repose in the Living Father."

152 Salome said, "When the Lord spoke of the first being the last and the last being the first, he was speaking of the Bridegroom and Holy Bride."

153 Mary said, "If the being is separate from the becoming, then there is no life in the becoming; and if the becoming is separate from the being, then the being does not exist. Being and becoming are one, for it is written: 'The Lord and His Name are One.'"

154 Mary said, "If you believe in a multiplicity of gods, it is inferior; yet if you do not recognize the many powers, superior knowledge is impossible."

155 Some young women among the disciples asked Mary, "When you knew the Lord, what was it like?" Mary said, "Why do you ask of what has passed away when this knowledge is in your presence?"

156 Mary said, "When new life comes to you, do not cling to the old."

157 Mary said, "An angel led Lot's wife to life, but she turned to gaze at destruction and became what was dead. When the angel leads you out of the corruption of the world, do not turn toward the world again as she did."

158 Mary said to her disciples, "Do not be deceived by the name 'Comforter' that is given to the Holy Spirit. Before she is the Comforter, her name is Deep Trouble, and she will seem as an angel of wrath before appearing as an angel of mercy."

159 Mary said, "To fear death is to fear life, and those who fear death are not alive. It is for this reason they fear death—they fear to know who and what they are."

160 Mary said, "There is heart and soul, mind and life, and there is Light; let all of these be united in the Light and they will become the Light—the Living Yeshua is proof of this."

161 Mary said, "Those who say Christ was crucified do not know what they are saying, and those who say Christ was not crucified also do not know what they are saying. Those who have many words concerning the crucifixion are ignorant of the Anointed, for the truth of the Anointed is the Risen Savior, the Bornless One."

162 Mary said, "There are twelve gates through which souls enter into the world, but one gate through which all depart. Yet that one gate is many, for it opens above and below and again into the world. When you pass through it, remember to gather yourself and rise up, and join yourself to what appears. Do not fear white brilliance, for it will deliver you."

163 Mary said, "No one will explain the Lord to another person, but the Spirit will explain everything and the Lord will speak to those who have ears to hear."

164 Mary said to her disciples, "Do not speak of deep things until you know the simple, and when you know the simple, do not neglect the things of depth."

165 Mary said, "The archons thought that they killed the Christ, just as they thought by their own power they created the world and humanity. But they were self-deluded, for they crushed only an empty husk, like themselves, and they began their own end in so doing!"

166 Mary said, "The Anointed is the Light-presence above the cross and in the cross, and if the Light was in the image, it did not shine forth until the resurrection. You also have the Light above you and in you, though it is concealed. Seek to bring it forth and let it shine, so that your image above and below might be complete. Then you will be free forever and ever."

167 Mary said to her companions, "This I am, of which the Lord spoke, this is you and the kingdom and the power and the glory; it is everyone and everything. And so it is!"

168 Mary said, "When the wind blows, listen, the Spirit is speaking; let your prayers be set upon the four winds in Spirit so that they should be a blessing to the whole earth. If you pray in this way, the Supreme Spirit above will receive your prayer."

169 Mary said, "If you have all knowledge but lack love, then you lack knowledge altogether."

170 Mary said, "We speak in the tongues of angels and beasts and the ancient ones, yet only human beings hear and understand our wisdom."

171 Mary said, "If the Truth is in you, but you do not speak it, how can you be true? When will your perfection come?"

172 Mary said, "Guard your intention and be willful in love; for it is the intention of any activity which is its truth. Many do the right things with wrong intentions and are taken down into the infernal abodes, and there are those who appear to do what is wrong but have entered into the Great Ascension."

173 Mary said, "There are great and shining ones who come among you. Be careful in your dealings with others, for truly, you may not know that one who comes before you is among these divine powers. Live as one among the righteous ones and angels, for it may be you do not know the divine power in you."

174 Mary said, "Beware of those who glorify and bear witness of themselves, for all who are true have heralds and the Holy Spirit is the True Witness."

175 Mary said, "If a person says, 'I found it,' know that they do not have it; yet if a person does not believe they have it, they will never find it."

176 Mary said, "Be careful with the names, for there is great power in them. Yet, unless the great power is in you, they are nothing."

177 Mary said, "Seventy-two angels compose the Name, yet even the angels did not know how to speak it until the Logos came to be below."

178 Mary said to some of her disciples, "No one was alive until the Anointed came. Now there are the dead and there are the living ones."

179 Mary said, "If you desire Truth, it will be disclosed to you, but if it is not disclosed then you do not desire it. If you desire Truth, then your desire is the manifestation of the Spirit of Truth you seek, and that desire is self-fulfilling and self-generating, and one who has it will become the self-begotten One."

180 Mary said, "There is death everywhere below, but there is life above. Bring down your life that you might have the power to raise the dead, even as the Lord raised our brother."

181 A disciple asked Mary, "When the Lord raised Lazarus, where did Lazarus go?" Mary said, "Like the Baptist, he is a secretive and wild spirit; only the Holy Spirit knows where he went, for she hides him as the witness for the End-Of-Days. And so he lives and shall live to bear witness to everything, even as the Lord spoke of him."

182 Mary was speaking to her disciples and they were marveling at the mysteries pouring forth from her. She said to them, "If anyone speaks a mystery and reveals it, it is not the person who has spoken, but the Spirit in the person."

183 Mary said, "One who has life can give life, but one who is dead cannot even help him or herself. Acquire life so that you have life to give."

184 Mary said, "Everything that is the Lord's belongs to me and everything that is mine belongs to him. It is this way with all who love the Lord."

185 Mary said, "Considering all things that have transpired, do not grasp at answers but live in holy awe and wonder. In this way, all things are made known."

186 Mary said, "There was no life in this body until I met the Lord, but then I received my life. And now I rejoice in the Lord of Life, the Holy One who dances with me and I with him."

187 Some disciples asked Mary, "Should we be celibate?" Mary said, "Be what you are, and inwardly be like unto the holy angels."

188 A woman said to Mary, "I do not wish to have a child, so as not to give birth to a slave." Mary said to her, "Blessed are you when you do not do so!" Another woman hearing this became troubled, and she said to Mary, "But Mary, I long to have a child who might labor for the kingdom." Mary said to her, "Blessed are you when you have such a child in your arms!"

189 Mary said, "Many are concerned with unreal things, but as for you, pay attention to the real. What is real is in your heart, and therein you will know it. What is on the outside is unreal, but what is on the inside is real. When you join the inside and outside, above and below, then the whole is real."

190 Mary said, "Stay always with the zeal and love you had at first, and you will not err, for such is the way of a child of God."

191 Mary said, "Even when the Lord laid himself down, he did not sleep nor cease from his labor, and even now he labors in you in the Spirit. So labor continually with him and you shall savor the fruits of this divine labor."

192 Mary spoke with her disciples, and she said, "Men think that the Lord came to save the world, but he did not come to save the world. The Anointed has come as a force of fire and light to shatter and burn the world utterly away, until only Truth remains in it."

193 Some disciples inquired of Mary about the end of time. Mary said, "It is the Day of Understanding. In that time, there will be holy apostles who bring the knowledge of the covenant of the Mother Spirit, and there will be many false prophets in the world. A great Light and great darkness shall enter into the world, and great conflict and confusion will follow. The Bride will be with the holy ones and she will bring with her two witnesses, and there will be many signs in the matrix of the world, and also there will be wonders, though hidden. If peace is attained before that time, then all shall come to pass by way of pure grace; yet in those days, if peace is not attained, then grace shall surely appear as woes and wrath. On account of the archons, it is unlikely that peace shall be attained before that day. But the holy shall be set apart, and though they die yet shall they live to enter the bridal chamber."

194   Mary said, "In the day of the coming of the Anointed, many shall look and see, and among them many will be unwilling to enter the Light, for they shall not recognize the Light in the Daughter sent among them."

195   Mary said, "One who knows the Mother is near to the Father, but one who denies the Mother is far from the Father. There is not two, but only one God, and God is both Father and Mother."

196   Mary said, "The name of the Anointed is not the name men speak, but it is a name sealed in the heart of the elect, and because they are holy when they speak it, no one hears it, save for those who are elect."

197   Mary said, "Listen! The Holy Spirit is supernal, yet she is everywhere here below. She is the light of the heavens and the fire of Gehenna, and she is the Life-power in all creatures in heaven and earth and beneath the earth—she is the All-In-All. If anyone is ignorant of her, then they are surely not alive."

198   Mary said, "The Way is narrow, for there is but one Path for each soul, and the unique essence of the soul is the Way, Truth, and Light. Save that one lives by way of this, one will not come into life."

199   Mary said, "Let divine passion play upon you, and let the Spirit carry you where she will; then you will know what divine rapture is."

200 Mary said to her disciples, "At the dawn of the End-of-Days, many wisdom treasuries shall be discovered, and there will be many who receive the light of those days; yet, on account of the great darkness, there will be a multitude of false lights and all manner of deceptions. Before the greater joy, I tell you, great sorrow and suffering will engulf the world. Yet, all shall be as it is to be, and all things shall be accomplished."

201 Mary said, "Live as though the Lord is coming tomorrow and you will not go wrong."

202 Mary said, "The meaning of repentance is this: If you miss the mark, adjust your aim. A baptism is given for the remission of sin, so that the soul might be loosed from the bow aimed at the Supernal Abode."

203 Mary said, "God Most High became Mother and Father to conceive and give birth to the Son and Holy Spirit. And so God formed the primordial womb from which to give birth to the image and likeness of Godself. Those who know the Virgin Mother will also experience the conception of Christ, and the Holy Spirit will manifest as them."

204 Mary said, "I said to the Lord, 'Let me know you,' and the Lord said to me, 'As you wish, know yourself.'"

205 Mary said, "If you do not know yourself, how will you propose to know God?"

206 Mary said, "I am the aura of flames dancing about him, and he is the center of Light—I am everywhere, but he is nowhere; I am he and he is me. There is no difference from beginning to end. Know the Lord, the One Anointed with the Supernal Light of God and you will come into the acquaintance of Holy Fire."

207 Mary said, "Moses saw a burning bush; but I tell you, in the Spirit of the Anointed we have beheld the entirety on fire!"

208 Mary said, "All were in the bondage of slavery, under the dominion of Pharaoh, until the Anointed came. But since the

Anointed came, we have become free men and women, and we have been set over the taskmasters. The law is prophecy; the Gospel is the fulfillment of prophecy. Yet, to the Aeon of the Bride and Mother Spirit, the Gospel that is with us is prophecy. Let those who have ears, listen and hear the Word and Wisdom of the Almighty!"

209 Mary said, "If you know how to cast the circle, then you will know how to deliver the spirits; for the secret of deliverance lies in the circle ascending."

210 Mary said, "The spark must become a flame, and the flame must become a blazing fire. When you shine like the sun, you will be complete."

211 Mary said, "The Supernal Light has not been seen in the world before the Anointed brought it down. Now there is a seed of Light and the fruition is forthcoming."

212 Mary said to her companions, "The ages and all that appears will pass away, but the Aeon of Perfect Light will remain. It is eternal."

213 Mary said, "Look! You are a shadow in the Light. Cleave to the Light and let the shadow pass away."

214 A woman asked Mary, "How can a woman be holy?" Mary said, "The man who is holy knows he is no man; therefore, it is the same for a woman. Those who see male and female see only an appearance, for inwardly there is neither female nor male. These appearances are like shadows, and those who grasp at shadows and do not look to the Light miss the mark of Truth."

And again, Mary said, "The Mother and the Bride and She-Who-Is-Wise is within every woman, just as the Father and the Son are within every man; the human being is holy when in possession of her or his humanity."

215 Mary said, "Many are the wisdom treasuries that are hidden, awaiting their discovery. If you court Wisdom, she will give you her dowry and all that is in her house will become yours."

216 Mary said, "Wisdom seeks true lovers and goes to those who seek her. No one will lack Wisdom if in their heart they yearn for her."

217 Mary said, "Many are the false lights. If the True Light had not come and Grace did not open the way, no one would have escaped deception."

218 Mary said to her disciples, "Here something precious is revealed by concealing it, but in the world-to-come it will be revealed by revealing it. Look and see!"

219 Mary said, "Many are they who wander aimless and are bound to missing the mark. It is unbecoming for a human being to live without purpose. For this reason the Lord has taught us to live in a purposeful way and has given us an aim, and he is our purpose and our aim—the Risen One."

220 Mary said, "It may be that a fool is wiser than an intelligent person, for the fool is more likely to know that whatever intelligence arises comes from God."

221 Mary said, "It is, indeed, difficult for a wealthy person to enter into the kingdom of heaven, for the wealthy are like the archons, believing they have created on their own and that the power is their own, though it is not. Yet, the wealthy person who serves the kingdom with their wealth shall be rich in the kingdom of heaven."

222 Mary said, "Every blessing is received inwardly. If one receives an apostle and is blessed, one receives the blessings of an apostle. If one receives a prophet or a righteous person and is blessed, then one receives the blessing of the prophet or righteous person. And so it is with every blessing one may receive, one receives inwardly and one is received."

223 Mary said, "Many say that they have received the Anointed, but one cannot receive unless one is received. Therefore, seek to be received to that you might receive and give, and Grace will accomplish everything within you."

224 Mary taught her disciples, saying, "Be certain to acquire your light-image so that you might be seen in the Living Father and your name may appear in the Book of Life."

225 Mary said, "Yahweh is passing by, therefore Yahweh is seen. Otherwise, no one would ever see the Great Spirit."

226 Mary said, "This world is a shadow of the World of Truth, and yet there is a great blessing in it. Here, there is time to recognize error from truth and to enact the truth, as though a pause to change your heart and mind. But when death comes and the soul departs the body, nothing can be changed."

227 Mary said to her chosen ones, "In the Supernal Realm, it is clear who has come into being and who is unbecoming, for the images of the elect shine brightly, but the beasts of the field do not appear."

228 Mary said, "Souls exchange sparks with one another and we carry sparks of one another and are connected in this way. Be certain to give to everyone what is theirs and to receive what is yours so that all are complete."

229 Mary said, "Nothing here shall remain. See that you also go your way."

230 Mary said to her companions, "Do you have money?" They said to her, "Yes, we have money." She said to them, "Good! Be certain to pay the ransom and buy a staff for the journey."

231 Mary spoke, and she said, "When you pray, let your heart abide in its place, and if it runs, let it return to its abode, which is the Risen Savior."

232 Mary said, "If you become empty, the Lord will give himself to you in full; if you lose yourself, you will acquire the Holy Spirit."

233 Mary said, "Angels appear in the world along with human beings, but the Perfect Human Being is superior to all angels. Have you not heard of Enoch who walked with Yahweh and was taken up in divine rapture? Every true initiate is set above

the angels, because she or he has knowledge of the name of God."

234 Mary said, "Today, you are lower than the angels, though some among you are equal to them. When you are complete, you will be above them."

235 Mary said, "Time is nothing, eternity is everything. Be clear about this!"

236 Mary said, "Who has ever heard of a pregnant mother unwilling to give birth in her time? May you also be willing to give birth to your soul when called out of the body. For your body is the Virgin Mother giving birth to your soul in the Eternal Abode."

237 Mary was speaking, and she said, "Words have no meaning apart from the Mother Spirit, therefore to know her is meaningful. Words have meaning to the extent that they invoke knowledge of her, but she is known only in silence."

238 Mary said, "Be conscious of your speech, for among human beings it is the greatest blessing and greatest curse. It binds and it liberates. Be liberating with your speaking and beware not to bind yourself and others."

239 Mary said, "There is a mystery to be played out through manhood and womanhood, yet, truly I tell you, it is concealed by male and female."

240 Mary said, "The Lord of Initiation has passed by. See that you receive initiation and bring it to fullness."

241 Mary said, "What appears divided has never been separated, yet division appears for the sake of love and the perfection of will, so that in unification a greater joy should come to pass. If there is sorrow it shall pass away like the shadows of night on the Day of Be-With-Us."

242 Mary said, "The body is a corpse and yet it lives for a while. While it is alive, it is the temple of a great presence, for your soul is in it and the Anointed indwells your soul."

243 Mary said, "The essence of the Light is transparent, it is the Holy Virgin; when you become transparent, you will be united with her and attain the perfection of your freedom."

244 Mary said, "The true elements are hidden by the visible, so also are the true rites of the Gospel hidden by the visible. Look to see what is hidden and you will understand."

245 Mary said, "When the circle is engraved and the fire is lit and blazing, invoking the name of the Lord and the shining ones, offer everything into the holy fire as into the Shekinah of God."

246 Mary said. "Many seek the resurrection of the flesh, but the superior resurrection is of the Spirit and is eternal. Seek always that which is superior."

247 Mary said, "If the body is to be raised up, then the body must be transformed; and so it is with everything below. But when things below are transformed, they are no longer of the world, though they may appear in it, and when they disappear they will not appear again."

248 Mary said, "The Lord has called us to gather in, not to scatter and disperse."

249 Mary said to her companions, "In the Anointed, Eve and Lilith are redeemed, for the Logos entered for the sake of the salvation of Sophia, and she is lifted up in him to her proper abode. Lilith is the power of Eve and Eve is the perfection of Lilith, so that, joined, they are True Womanhood. Eve united in herself, and Adam and Eve united in one another, is the image of the Second Adam that appears in the bridal chamber. Therefore, manhood and womanhood are perfected and made complete in one another—so it was ordained from the beginning and so it shall be in the end."

250 Mary said, "Saint and sinner are appearances, but the Truth and Light is beyond. In the Anointed there is neither saint nor sinner, but only the Righteous One. Therefore, do what is right according to the soul of Light in you and you will be counted among the righteous and elect. We will meet again in the Supernal Abode on the Day of Be-With-Us."

This is the Gospel of the Sophia of Ain Sof (One-Without-End), for there is no end to the divine revelation transpiring through the Holy Bride. Whatever might be spoken or written, there is always much more to be received. To all who listen and hear in the Spirit, she continues to speak. The Gospel of Sophia will only be complete at the time of the Second Coming—the Reception of the Bride and the Age of the Mother Spirit. Amen.

CONCLUSION

An Entrance into the Gnostic Experience

As the Gnostic legends of St. Mary Magdalene reflect, Lady Mary is the inmost disciple of Lord Yeshua. She is his wife and divine consort. She serves as the Christ-bearer with him and is co-preacher of the Gospel with him. She becomes the First Apostle of the Risen Savior—the foundation of the apostolic succession and the true Holy Church. Indeed, just as Lord Yeshua is the living temple of the Divine presence and power, so also is she; and according to Gnostic teachings, we are also to be living temples of God's presence and power; hence sons and daughters of God.

Essentially, Gnosticism is a path of self-realization through a direct spiritual or mystical experience of the Risen Savior and Holy Bride—hence the recognition and realization of the Light-presence (Christ-presence) in us and conscious unification with God. In the Gnostic experience, the Risen Savior and Holy Bride are a distinct Divine presence and power. The aim of the Gnostic Christian is to embody that Divine presence and power. Thus, Gnosticism is based upon a spiritual life and spiritual practice through which we create the conditions necessary for a spiritual or mystical experience of the Truth and Light. Once established in the Gnostic experience, we seek to live according to the Spirit of Truth revealed in our own experience. In so doing, with Lord Yeshua we may say, "...we speak of what we know and testify to what we have seen..." (Gospel of St. John 3:11).

The issue for the Gnostic is not dogmatic creeds and doctrines to be blindly believed and adhered to. Rather, the issue is the reception of spiritual teachings and practices through which gnosis might be made manifest. Gnostic legends, stories,

and sayings of the oral tradition are one of the ways Gnostic teachings and practices are communicated. If we contemplate and meditate
upon the legends, aware of the symbolic and mystical language from
which they are woven, we swiftly discover deeper spiritual meanings
within them. At the same time, because these stories and sayings arise
from the realization experience of Gnostic elders and tau (adepts and
masters), as much as communicating teachings and practices, they
also communicate spiritual energy—hence something of the Divine
presence and power of which they speak. In the case of the Gnostic
legends of St. Mary Magdalene, they invoke and communicate the
presence and power of the Holy Bride—the female emanation of the
Christos, Christ the Sophia (Wisdom). Thus, we may contemplate
and meditate upon the Gnostic legends, seeking to draw out the secret knowledge of the teachings and practices contained in them; or
we may study and contemplate them with the intention of invoking
the Divine presence and power of the Holy Bride, and thus focus on
something more experiential than conceptual. Ultimately, it is the experiential level that Gnostics value the most, for it is the experiential
level that leads to the enlightenment and liberation experience—Divine Gnosis.

The presence and power of the Holy Bride is very real in the experience of a Sophian Gnostic, as is the experience of the Living Yeshua
or Risen Savior. If one opens one's mind and heart to her, inviting and
welcoming her presence into oneself and one's life, then she will enter
and reveal herself as Christ the Sophia. Through her, one will acquire
gnosis of the Holy Bride and Risen Savior joined in mystical union
with God. Truly, one will find that she is as near as one's own body.
More than imparting the Gnostic and Light-transmission through
philosophical arguments and concepts, she will impart the Spirit of
Truth through one's own life experiences. Cleaving to the Holy Bride,
one will know the Risen Savior within and beyond oneself and perchance experience supernal or Messianic consciousness—hence enlightenment and liberation. Indeed! For the devotee of the Bride, life
becomes the vehicle of the Great Ascension!

Along with contemplation and meditation on the Gnostic legends
of St. Mary Magdalene, following are some spiritual practices com-

monly given to Sophian initiates. Through these practices, one can come into contact with the Holy Bride and bring her into one's life on a more experiential level.

The Holy Bride in Spiritual Life and Practice

Meditation with the Holy Bride

The masters of the Tradition have said, "If you meditate on the Holy Bride, she will reveal herself; if you envision her, she will come to you." Whenever you wish to meditate upon her, sit where you will not be disturbed, and let your body find its own natural rhythm of breath. Gently focus upon your breath; let go of the dream-like past and fantasies of futures yet to be—bring yourself into the present moment, where you are and the Anointed Bride is.

Once you have brought yourself into the moment and have settled in, envision a spiritual sun shining in your heart and gather yourself into it. Let go of the surface consciousness and all tension, stress or negativity. Let go of your self-identify with name and form, and identify yourself with the Light-presence in you. Go within, into the depths of your heart, and abide in the Light.

When you have centered yourself in this way, envision a ray of light shooting out of your heart and magically transforming into the image of the Holy Bride, which hovers in the space before you. Her feet do not touch the ground; she dances in the sky. Her inner robe is white brilliance, her outer robe is crimson red, and there is a crimson red shawl over her head. Her eyes are green, her skin an olive complexion, and she is most exquisite to behold. She holds the jar of anointing in her hands, with which she anointed the Lord. There is a golden aura about her and a rainbow aura beyond that. There are wounds of stigmata on her body and brilliant light pours from them. The entire image is formed of translucent light, akin to the image of a rainbow in the sky. Meditate on this image of Our Lady and commune with her.

As you meditate upon the image of the Bride, see her smiling upon you and know her blessing you and receiving you, as you receive her. Envision that she anoints you as her own. Receive her as you own and know that you are received by the Lord through her. Envision that, when she anoints you, she pours out fluid light from her jar and that the light pours over you and into you. See her blessing you with light emanations from her body and aura of all colors of rays. See yourself becoming self-radiant like her, until you also shine with light and are enshrouded with a great aura of light. Know that you are whole and complete as you are in her and she in you, and that whatever your heart's desire is, it is already fulfilled in the Holy Bride.

When your communion with the Anointed Bride is complete, take up her simple chant: *Kallah Messiah* (all short vowel sounds). As you chant, merge with the sound-vibration of her holy name. When you are about to conclude the chant, envision her image dissolving into fluid light, and as you fall silent, envision she pours into your heart. Let your mind become her Christ Mind, your heart her Sacred Heart, and your body her Emanation Body. Know yourself at one with the Anointed Bride.

As you walk in the world, see all that appears as her Palace of Lights, hear every sound as her Voice or Word, receive all thoughts and emotions arising in the mind as the spontaneous expression of her Innate Wisdom. In this way, walk as the Anointed Bride and walk with the Anointed Bride throughout the day. If you meditate on the Bride each day and live in this holy awareness, you will acquire intimate gnosis of our Lady, St. Mary Magdalene.

The Holy Fire

This meditation is the same as the above in the beginning and end, but the image of the Bride transforms into a dancing flame of fire, dancing around you and through you, purifying and consecrating you. It may be impossible to sit still. So if you are inspired to do so, arise and move and dance with the Bride, progressively entering into the most intimate embrace, until she is you and you are her. Let yourself be burned utterly away in the flames of Divine passion!

Sophia Nigrans

The outer image of Sophia Nigrans (Dark Wisdom) is a beautiful Nubian woman, though she may also appear as a crazy old black woman, as though a hag. Her chant is the chant of Lilith: *Allah Lala Lalil Lola Lalu Lilatu* (or one may use her simple chant—*Kali Kallah*). When she comes, she is wild and unpredictable. Though no pronunciation of her chant can be openly given, like herself, it reveals itself to those who take it up. The new moon is the ideal time for her invocation and meditation—the time of purification, revelation, new conception, and initiation. If you seek gnosis of mystical death and spiritual rebirth, or seek a greater flow of creativity, or find yourself in need of deep healing, then you might wish to try this invocation and meditate on the Black Bride. It is especially powerful for women seeking empowerment in life and spirit, and for men seeking the necessary understanding to be partners with empowered and independent women. (In the Sophian Tradition, Lilith represents our reclaiming essential aspects of the Sacred Feminine and womanhood that have been rejected and demonized—aspects necessary to the fullness of life and self-realization.)

The Shrine

If you create a shrine to the Holy Bride in your home and offer candles and incense to the Great Spirit upon it, the presence of the Anointed Bride will be in your home and she will come and visit you. This is a simple way to honor her and it creates a perfect spot for prayer and meditation.

Music, Song, and Dance

Encountering the Holy Bride can be very simple and direct. All you need to do is hold her in your mind, cleave to her in your heart, delight in music, song, and dance, and you will come to know her. You will experience her within and all around you, for she will be your joy and your joy will be hers.

The Circle

Gather with some women. Share your stories and stories of the Bride with one another, and the spirit of St. Mary Magdalene will be present with you. Indeed! Gather together for creative expression, with stories, poetry, song, and dance for one another, and the spirit of the Bride will be among you. Whenever a circle or gathering is consecrated to our

Lady of Gnosis, she is present in that place. If there are men willing to enter into the circle with women in celebration of the Holy Bride, so much the better—for then the truth of Bride and Groom will be manifest.

The Feast of the Holy Bride

In the Sophian Tradition, May 1st is the Feast of the Holy Bride. Gathering and celebrating a feast, telling her stories, offering creative expressions, celebrating life, light, love, and liberty through music, song and dance, you can create a ceremony honoring the Anointed Bride on her holy day. You can do this alone or with spiritual friends.

(These practices are seeds which, when creatively cultivated and nurtured, will lead to experiences and gnosis of the Anointed Bride. There is no "right" way, only the way that works for you. Truly, her meditations and worship are a creative affair.)

A Closing Word and Prayer

With the dawn of male-dominated orthodoxy and fundamentalism, which occurred some 300 to 400 years into the Christian movement, and the complete rejection that followed of the Holy Bride, St. Mary of Magdal, the deeper mystical and magical elements of Christianity were rejected. I dare say the true spirit and soul of the Christ revelation was lost to the majority of Christians.

Today, we can only wonder what the face of Christianity and our Western societies and cultures would look like had the Holy Bride been well received and the Sacred Feminine remained a central part of Christianity. Of course, we cannot go back in time and undo the injustice and harm that has been done, but we can actively seek to reclaim the Sacred Feminine and restore the Holy Bride to her rightful place alongside the Bridegroom, seeking a more holistic and integral Christianity. Indeed! Given the extreme imbalance between the masculine and feminine in our present human condition and world and the evolutionary crisis we are facing, the need to reclaim the Sacred Feminine and to restore the Holy Bride to her rightful place is clear. When we seek to reclaim the Sacred Feminine in our spiritual quest and to actively invoke the Holy Bride, we do so not only for ourselves, but for the sake of humanity and the world. According to the Sophian vision of the Christ revelation, it is the coequality and mystical union of the masculine and feminine that is the spiritual hope for the future of humanity and Planet Earth.

In closing, let us pray:

Heavenly Father, Earthly Mother, may the Holy Bride be received and may the dawn of the Age of the Mother Spirit come; may the fullness of the Truth and Light shine among us, the image of the Bridegroom and Holy Bride in the bridal chamber! Amen.

GLOSSARY

Adam Ha-Rishon: Literally, the "first adam"; the supernal or Divine human being; the androgynous archetype of humanity, including the potential of both male and female. *See also* Second Adam.

Adam Kadmon: Literally, "the primordial Adam" or "primordial human being"; the first universe or world of emanation in the Kabbalah; the transcendent nature of the human soul inseparable from God and Godhead; the primordial root of the archetype of humanity (root of Adam Ha-Rishon). It is said that the Soul of the Messiah is the Soul of Adam Kadmon. (This principle is considered a supreme mystery in the Sophian teachings, one which is unthinkable and unspeakable but which may be glimpsed in peak states of higher consciousness.)

Adonai: Literally, "Lord"; a name of God; a divine name corresponding to Malkut or the Kingdom, which is the outermost Sefirot on the Kabbalistic Tree of Life; a name used in place of the Great Name, Yahweh; a name applied to an enlightened or Christed individual.

Aeon: Literally, "age," for example, the Age of Aquarius; the spiritual energy-intelligence of a thought-form or ideal in the spiritual world that influences trends of thought and events in the material world; an emanated aspect of Divine reality that influences the evolution of creatures and creation; a spiritual entity of great power and influence that may be divine, admixed, or dark. In Gnosticism, aeons are frequently spoken of as pairs, male and female, which serve to activate and balance one another. Typically, in Gnostic cosmology, there are both upper and lower aeons, the former being associated with the True Light and the latter with the demiurge. The lower aeons are generally considered distorted forms of the upper aeons due to the influence of cosmic ignorance. (This term represents a subtle and complex subject in Gnosticism, the teachings of which can radically differ from one Gnostic school to another.)

Aeon of the Holy Spirit: A Gnostic term for the Age of the Second Coming; a constant continuum of Divine inspiration to which the soul of Light has access.

Aeon of Truth: An emanation of Divine reality in which All-Truth is inwardly known; a state of True Gnosis; the awareness of supernal or Messianic consciousness; also considered an aspect of Mother Sophia.

Aeons of Light: Upper Divine aeons; aeons corresponding to the Light-emanations of the Supernal World; pure emanation of Divine reality; aeons transcendent of the dominion of the demiurge and archons.

Alien God: A common term in Gnosticism for the True Light or True God, or God beyond the demiurge. From the Gnostic perspective, until a soul awakens to its true nature—Light—God is unknown and therefore God is, in effect, an "alien" presence. The term implies that what is often worshipped as "God" in religion is not God, but the demiurge. It also implies that creation is largely the product of the demiurge—a restricted manifestation of Divine Being. *See* demiurge.

Anointed: Messiah or Christ; the Truth of the inmost part of the soul of Light in us; the Light-presence that is within everyone and everything; the Indweller of Light; a title typically applied to Lord Yeshua or to Lady Mary, but which may be applied to any Christed or enlightened person.

Apostle: A Light-bearer or Christ-bearer; a Christed or enlightened individual who teaches and initiates others; an elder or tau in Sophian Gnosticism; an initiate who embodies something of the Supernal Light.

Arayot: Teachings on a sensual and sexual mysticism in the Kabbalah; teachings in the Western Mystery Tradition akin to tantra in

Eastern Schools; teachings related to the mystery of hieros gamos or the sacred marriage.

Archons: Literally, "rulers"; great spiritual or cosmic forces under the dominion of the demiurge that are either admixed or dark and hostile; the spiritual or cosmic forces that dominate unenlightened society and the world; spiritual or cosmic forces of ignorance.

Babylon: A symbolic term for unenlightened society; a term for the material world devoid of the awareness of the spiritual world; a term for life dominated by the ego or the psychological condition of the egocentric state. (The same is true of "Egypt" in the symbolic and mystical language of Sophian Gnosticism.)

Baptism: A rite of initiation in Gnostic Christianity, which, although it may be performed as an outward ceremony, is understood as a completely inward experience of the Light and Spirit; an experience of a spiritual or mystical death and rebirth; an event of self-transformation or spiritual awakening; a rite of passage in Gnostic Christianity.

Beloved: A term used for both Lord Yeshua and Lady Mary in the Sophian Tradition.

Bet El: Literally, "house of God"; primarily, among Gnostics, this term indicates a person who embodies something of the Divine presence and power—hence, one who is a living temple.

Body of Light: The subtle body transformed by the influx of Supernal Light; Solar Body; Body of the Resurrection; a subtle body of enlightened or Christed consciousness; the mystical body of the Risen Savior.

Book of Enoch: Actually, the Book of Enoch is composed of three holy books that are not included in the canonized Bible, though they are mentioned by the Apostle Jude in his epistle that appears in the Bible; these sacred texts are often studied by Sophians. Also, a symbolic term among initiates for a "book of secret knowledge" that is not written but is transmitted as an oral tradition.

Book of Ratziel: A legendary book of Magical Kabbalah said to be in the custody of Ratziel, the archangel of Wisdom; a secret body of teachings in Sophian Gnosticism.

Bridal Chamber: The experience of a conscious unification with the Christos in God or with the Light-presence in the Light-continuum; the state of enlightenment or True Gnosis; the inmost mystery of hieros gamos or the sacred marriage; inmost secret teachings of the Arayot.

Bride: The most common term for St. Mary Magdalene in the Sophian Tradition, specifically the Holy Bride. A term for Malkut or the Kingdom on the Kabbalistic Tree of Life, specifically when Malkut is joined to Tiferet or Beauty, the Christ center on the Tree of Life. (See *Gnosis of the Cosmic Christ: A Gnostic Christian Kabbalah*, Llewellyn, 2005.)

Bridegroom: A common term for Lord Yeshua; a term for Tiferet or Beauty on the Kabbalistic Tree of Life.

Bright Sophia: See Sophia Stellarum.

Brother Azrael: The angel of death; a term connoting intimacy or familiarity with death; gnosis of the illusory quality of death; an archangel said to be associated with the rite of baptism—hence mystical death.

Chrism: Literally, "anointing"; a rite of initiation in Gnostic Christianity; the reception of an influx of Supernal Light; an experience of Divine Illumination.

Christos: Literally, "the Anointed"; the Light-presence or Christ-presence; the presence of awareness; the union of Logos and Sophia; the image of the bridal chamber.

Clear Light: The true nature of the Light; the bornless nature of consciousness; the primordial ground of consciousness; the inmost essence of the Supernal Light—hence Transparent Light, which is Keter or the Crown on the Kabbalistic Tree of Life. The same principle is also represented by the name "Melchizedek" in Sophian teachings.

Crazy Wisdom: A term for the way of teaching in the Sophian Tradition; Transcendental Wisdom; a state of Divine intoxication or Divine inspiration; also called "Divine Folly."

Crone: Grandmother, Old Woman, or Wise Woman; an aspect of the Divine Feminine that deals with transcendental wisdom and secret knowledge; the view of an illuminated initiate.

Crone of Ancient Wisdom: One of the seven aspects of the Holy Bride, St. Mary Magdalene.

Dark Sophia: See Sophia Nigrans; see also Lilith, Naamah, and Iggaret.

Daughter Sophia: The immanent aspect of Sophia in creation; the emanation of Mother Sophia in the lower worlds; Sophia in the realm of becoming; a title of St. Mary Magdalene as the Holy Bride; the aspect of Sophia that is redeemed/awakened by the incarnation of the Logos.

Demiurge (or Demiurgos): Literally, "false god," "false creator," or "lesser god." This is the principle of cosmic ignorance from which admixture and darkness enter into creation. The demiurge is often called the "dragon," the "unmaker," the "lord of forgetfulness" and "lord of cosmic illusion"—all of which give insight into Gnostic thought on the demiurge. Essentially, he is the chief of the archons, the shadow of which is called Satan in the Sophian Tradition. (Different trends of thought and names occur for the demiurge in the various Gnostic Traditions.)

Devekut: Literally, "cleaving" or "attachment"; a state of rapturous union; energized enthusiasm; mystical attainment.

Divine Kingdom: Synonymous with Light-kingdom; a state of Divine illumination; the awareness of Sacred Unity; the experience of life when Spirit-connected; a higher state of consciousness.

Dragon: A term denoting the Life-power when manifest under the dominion of the demiurge or cosmic ignorance; the dark side of the Force; raw energy of the cosmos; a force that flows through all things. Essentially, the "dragon" is the Spirit of Yahweh devoid of the awareness of Sacred Unity.

Earthly Mother: God in creation or the Divine presence and power in creation; one of the feminine aspects of Divine Being; the Matrix of the Divine Life on earth.

Elder: A Gnostic adept and teacher; principle teachers and guardians of Gnostic circles in the Sophian Tradition; a Gnostic apostle. (Elders and tau are not clergy in the Sophian Tradition, but are spiritual teachers and guides, akin to what one might find in Eastern Enlightenment Traditions.) See also Tau.

Elect: One who has received the Gnostic and Light-transmission; one chosen from among the faithful; the sons and daughters of Light; one who is guided from within; true mystics; one who has acquired gnosis; an initiate of the Interior Church.

El Elyon: Literally, "God most high"; Keter or the Crown on the Kabbalistic Tree of Life; the Alien God; the True Light; the transcendent aspect of God; the First Commandment according to the Gnostic Gospel, entitled Pistis Sophia.

Elohim: Literally, "one become many" or "one and many"; may also be translated as God/Goddess, as well as "gods and goddesses." It is a common name of God in the Bible and specifically represents God the Mother. Because the Divine Mother gives birth to all things in creation, including the demiurge, Elohim may also represent the demiurge, though typically it connotes the Divine Matrix within and behind creation. (The meaning of Elohim is very fluid in the Sophian Tradition and represents a complex Gnostic teaching on the nature of the Divine in creation.)

Entirety: Literally, "the All"; a Gnostic term for creation; sometimes this term may include the Pleroma, though often it does not.

Eternal Shabbat: The state of supernal or Messianic consciousness; the Divine Kingdom; the completion and fruition of creation; the world-to-come; the Supernal Abode.

Eve: Literally, the "mother of life"; the bright side of the feminine psyche; the "submissive woman"; the wise woman who initiates. The latter definition is most common to Gnosticism, as the Serpent in the Garden of Eden is often considered a personification of Sophia, from whom Eve receives the gift of the fiery-intelligence, which she then imparts to Adam. (Eve is a complex figure in Gnosticism, but is generally interpreted in a positive light in Sophian Gnosticism.)

Faith: An intuitive sense of an experience not yet had, which tends to invoke the experience; a sense of the mystery; an inner knowing of truth which remains as yet unconfirmed. In Gnosticism, it is not "blind belief" nor a mental or vital sentiment, but rather represents the power of an intuitive part of us, specifically of the soul.

Faithful: A term for religious individuals in whom the mystical inclination has not yet fully manifest; a term for a person of the outer and unspiritual church; a term for one who believes but has not yet attained gnosis; an intermediate stage in the development and evolution of the soul-being.

Fiery-Intelligence: The gift of the Holy Spirit that transforms the bestial human into the divine human; that which separates the beasts and humankind; that which makes a person spiritual or elect in the great work.

First Apostle: A title of St. Mary Magdalene who is the Apostle of the apostles in Sophian Gnosticism; the Holy Spirit power in the apostolic succession of Gnostic Tradition.

First Circle: The sacred circle of Lord Yeshua and Lady Mary. In honor of the Sacred Feminine, rather than the term "church," Sophians usually use the term "circle" to designate a Gnostic community.

Gabriel: Literally, "strength of God"; the divine herald; archangel corresponding to Yesod or the Foundation on the Kabbalistic Tree of Life; one of the seven archangels of the Christos according to the tradition. Gabriel is associated with dreams, visions, and prophecy; also with the element of water and the moon.

Gehenna: The name of the garbage dump west of ancient Jerusalem; the Hebrew term for hell realms.

Gnosis: Literally, "knowledge" or "secret knowledge"; knowledge or insight acquired through direct spiritual or mystical experience; also a state of Divine illumination. *See also* True Gnosis.

Gnosis of Melchizedek: This is synonymous with the gnosis of the Risen Savior; a state of supernal or Messianic-consciousness; the state of enlightenment and liberation; also a body of inmost secret teachings in the Sophian Tradition. This is the inmost secret level of the Gnostic and Light-transmission.

Gnostic: A person who has acquired gnosis or who is a practitioner of Gnosticism. (The term may include both Christian and Pagan practitioners of Gnosticism.)

Gnostic Transmission: A transmission of secret knowledge through which gnosis might be made manifest; initiation into a Gnostic Tradition; a transmission of spiritual knowledge directly from the Holy Spirit.

Gnosticism: A path of mystical knowledge; an initiatory tradition; a way of secret knowledge; a path to self-realization or enlightenment; a path founded upon the Gnostic experience and a Gnostic Tradition—one that shares the principle Gnostic ideas, such as teachings on the demiurge and archons, and so forth.

Golgotha: Literally, Mount of Skulls; place of the crucifixion. However, in Gnostic Christianity this is also a symbolic term for the Crown Star or Center of Energy on top of the head of the subtle body (Crown "Chakra").

Gospel of Truth: This phrase does not indicate a written gospel, but rather the direct experience of the Truth and Light of the Gospel— hence the Gospel as understood through direct spiritual or mystical experience.

Grail: Legend has it that St. Mary Magdalene created this holy relic by placing the cup used at the last supper to Lord Yeshua's side and catching some of the blood and water that was flowing from his wound. However, in Gnostic Christianity, St. Mary Magdalene herself is considered the Holy Grail, the Sacred Feminine that makes whole, heals, and gives life. It is frequently interpreted as the heart of the Gnostic practitioner open to receive the influx of Supernal Light.

Great Luminous Assembly: This is the assembly of enlightened or Christed beings and angels of God that forms the mystical body of the Risen Savior—hence the Matrix of the Divine Order.

Great Mother: A term for God the Mother; the Divine Feminine in its entirety; also the Upper Shekinah of the Kabbalah and the divine name Elohim.

Great Name of God: A term for the Tetragrammaton or Yahweh.

Great Seth: A common term for the Christos in Sophian Gnosticism; light of the cross or fiery cross; the Son of the Human One; the perfect human being; the Sacred Tau.

Great Spirit: A Gnostic term for the True Light or True God; in Greek, Agatho Daimon; synonymous with the Bornless Spirit or Headless Spirit.

Great Void: Primordial unconsciousness; oblivion; the great abyss on the Kabbalistic Tree of Life; prism of the cosmic illusion-power; sometimes called the "jaws of the unmaker." This term may also be used to indicate the empty nature of things or the no-thingness from which all things arise.

Great Work: The process of the enlightenment and liberation of all living spirits and souls; synonymous with the harvest of souls.

Heavenly Father: The transcendent aspect of God and Godhead; a title of Hokmah in the Christian Kabbalah; an anthropomorphic phrase for the Light-continuum.

Highest of Life: A term indicating the attainment of supernal or Messianic-consciousness (Christ consciousness); a conscious unification with God and Godhead; a title of Hokmah on the Kabbalistic Tree of Life according to the Christian Kabbalah.

Holy Mountain (or Holy Mount): A symbolic term for a higher state of consciousness in Gnostic jargon; a term used to indicate the crown star or center in the subtle body (Crown "Chakra").

Holy Spirit: Considered feminine in Gnostic Christianity, it is associated with both the Divine Mother and the Holy Bride. The active presence and power of the Christos, Logos, and Sophia and is frequently called the Mother Spirit. In Sophian teachings, the terms fiery intelligence and Holy Spirit are basically synonymous.

Hua: The great angel of the Lord; the great angel of the Anointed; the union of the archangels Metatron and Sandalphon, which correspond to Keter (Crown) and Malkut (Kingdom) on the Kabbalistic Tree of Life; also called the angel of the Shekinah. This is the angelic form of the Christos, specifically the Cosmic Christ.

Iggaret: The Hag of Chaos; the darkest aspect of Sophia Nigrans; the consort of the Destroyer. Essentially, Sophia underlies all spiritual forces and all life, including darkness, chaos, and evil, and represents the divine purpose within and behind these cosmic principles. Therefore, the Dark Sophia is associated with them.

Initiation: A transmission of gnosis or Light-power that begins a new cycle in the development and evolution of the soul or consciousness; a shared experience between initiates that reveals or communicates secret knowledge of mysteries; an opening in consciousness to new and higher levels; a peak experience in consciousness.

Inner Order: An inner circle within a Gnostic community; a circle of adepts among Gnostics; a gathering of initiates guided by the Holy Spirit; the Order of the Rose Cross in Christian Gnosticism; inner sanctuaries of the mysteries in Western Mystery Tradition; a body of inner mystical teachings and practices.

Jeweled Wisdom Body: The subtle body manifest as the Body of Light; also a specific manifestation of the Body of Light in supernal or Messianic-consciousness. See Body of Light.

Kabbalah: Literally, the "Tradition"; Jewish mysticism, which has become the foundation for several schools of Christian Gnosticism and mysticism; an ancient teaching of the path to enlightenment within Judeo-Christian Tradition.

Kallah Messiah: Literally, "Anointed Bride"; a name of St. Mary Magdalene indicating that she was Christed and coequal with Yeshua Messiah; the name of Lady Mary as the divine consort of Yeshua; the name of Christ in the Second Coming according to Sophian Gnostics.

Kamael: Literally, "burner of God"; archangel corresponding to Gevurah or Judgment on the Kabbalistic Tree of Life; archangel set over the order of the Seraphim. Kamael is called the "champion of God" and is associated with the planetary sphere of mars and the wrathful face of the Divine. He is one of the seven archangels of the Christos in Gnostic Christianity.

Kerubim: Literally, "strong ones"; the order of angels over which Gabriel presides.

Lady in Red: A name of St. Mary Magdalene as the Holy Bride.

Leviathan: Literally, "destruction"; called the Great Dragon; the arch demon associated with the western quarter of the sacred circle. (Teachings regarding Leviathan in Christian Gnosticism are distinctly esoteric and complex.) *See also* Dragon.

Light-continuum: The true nature of reality; Divine reality; the Pleroma of Light; the World of Supernal Light; the divine name Yahweh; the Heavenly Father.

Light-emanations: This is a common term for the Sefirot of the Kabbalistic Tree of Life in Gnostic Christianity. They are various gradations of the emanation of Supernal Light from the least to most restricted manifestations and represent the underlying metaphysical structure of creation.

Light-presence: A common Gnostic term for the Christos.

Light-transmission: There are many grades of the Light-transmission; however, basically, it is a spiritual or mystical experience in which one recognizes oneself as a person of Light who has come from the Light-continuum and is a direct spiritual or mystical experience of the Light-continuum. It is a term used to indicate the enlightenment experience of Christ consciousness.

Lilith (also Lilatu): Mistress of the Night; Sophia Nigrans; the dark side of Daughter Sophia or the Holy Bride; the dark side of the feminine psyche; the "rebellious or independent woman"; the power of the mystical death that leads to rebirth; a wrathful aspect of Sophia (or wrathful aspect of the Shekinah); a liberating aspect of Sophia. According to tradition, Eve and Lilith were joined as one in Lady Mary, which together represent the fullness and perfection of true womanhood.

Living Father: A term for the Life-power; synonymous with Great Spirit. *See also* Heavenly Father.

Living One: A name of the Risen Savior

Living Yeshua: Synonymous with the phrase Risen Savior; the Light-presence within Yeshua or anyone who embodies the Christos.

Logos: The Word of God; the sound-vibration underlying all things; the activating principle of the Christos; Divine Reason or Intelligence; the active manifestation of the Life-power; the principle of Divine illumination.

Magdal: The place where, according to legend, the Holy Bride was born; hence Mary of Magdal or Mary Magdalene.

Maiden: A youthful, energetic, and playful aspect of the Divine Feminine; purity of the Divine Feminine; the potential of the Divine Feminine. The Maiden may also represent the trickster-prankster-fool aspect of the Divine Feminine according to Sophian teachings.

Maiden of Light: One of the seven aspects of the Holy Bride; the energetic, inspirational, and illuminating aspect of Daughter Sophia.

Master of the Assembly: A Tau in Gnosticism; the head of the assembly of prophets—Baal Shem, Master of the Name; the thirteenth living apostle who is said to be the Master of the Apostolic Succession in a generation.

Melchizedek: Literally, "King of Righteousness"; the bornless nature of the soul or consciousness; the state of enlightenment and liberation; supernal or Messianic-consciousness; an enlightened individual. (In the Sophian Tradition, the inmost secret teachings and practices are called the Melchizedek Teachings.)

Messiah: Literally, "Anointed"; one who is anointed with the Supernal Light of God; an enlightened and liberated individual, as in the term Buddha in Eastern Schools; synonymous with Christ.

Metatron: The archangel of Keter (Crown) on the Kabbalistic Tree of Life; the name of Enoch after his divine rapture and translation into an angelic form according to legend; the greatest of all archangels, having dominion over the order of Hayyot Ha-Kodesh (Holy Living Creatures); archangel of supernal or Messianic-consciousness; master of the mysteries among the great angels of God.

Michael: Literally, "who is like unto God"; corresponds to Hod (Splendor) on the Kabbalistic Tree of Life; one of the seven archangels of the Christos. Michael has dominion over the order of Beni Elohim (sons of God) and is associated with the planetary sphere of Mercury and the element of fire.

Miriam's Well: An ancient symbol of the Divine Feminine that may connote Binah (Understanding) or Malkut (Kingdom) on the Kabbalistic Tree of Life. This is the legendary well that appeared wherever the Israelites wandered in the wilderness so long as the prophetess Miriam lived among them. According to tradition, it gave forth its waters when Miriam and twelve elder women would go out and sing heart songs to the Shekinah.

Mother of Life: A name for both Eve and Mary Magdalene as personifications of Sophia.

Mother of the Royal Blood: One of the seven aspects of St. Mary Magdalene as the personification of Sophia; a title indicating the royal bloodline of Yeshua born through Mary Magdalene; also a title of Mary Magdalene as the Apostle of Apostles or First Apostle.

Mother Sophia: The transcendental aspect of Sophia; Sophia of the upper worlds and aeons of Light; Sophia of the World of Supernal Light; the Divine Mother; cosmic and primordial Wisdom; God the Mother; the Great Mother.

Mother Spirit: *See also* Holy Spirit.

Mount of Olives: A term for the rite of Chrism; a symbolic term for the state of consciousness in which the Gnostic and Light-transmission occurs and gnosis is made manifest; any place the Light-transmission occurs.

Naamah: The queen of demons; one of the seven aspects of Daughter Sophia; an aspect of Sophia Nigrans; the Wisdom that liberates from negativity and demons. See Sophia Nigrans.

New Jerusalem: The Supernal Abode; the Light-kingdom; a name of the Holy Bride; Malkut (Kingdom) of Atzilut (Emanation) on the Kabbalistic Tree of Life; the state of consciousness experienced in the ascension, according to Gnostic jargon.

One-Without-End: Ain Sof, the Infinite; a common name of God in Kabbalah and Sophian Gnosticism. (See *Gnosis of the Cosmic Christ: A Gnostic Christian Kabbalah.*)

Order of Melchizedek: The primordial tradition; the secret order; the universal order of enlightenment; the divine order of the enlightened or Christed ones.

Order of St. Michael: An esoteric order associated with the guardianship and mysteries of the lineage of the royal blood (sangraal), as well as guardianship of reincarnations of St. Mary Magdalene.

Original Blessing: This is the state of the conception of souls and of life—the sacredness of human relationship, specifically the union of male and female in the bonds of love. The state of the androgynous one—human one. In Sophian teachings, we are born by way of an original blessing, not "original sin."

Outer Church (or Unspiritual Church): A Gnostic term for orthodox and fundamental forms of Christianity.

Outer Order: The outer circle of a Gnostic community; the outer body of teachings of a Gnostic Tradition.

Palace of Lights: A term for the Light-emanations of the Supernal World; a term for the divine name Elohim.

Perfect Aeon: A term for the union of Logos and Sophia; the Supernal aeon; the aeon of Truth-consciousness; eternal life; a continuity of awareness throughout all states of consciousness; the state of enlightenment.

Pleroma: Literally, "fullness"; a term for the infinite potential of God; the upper worlds or spiritual world; the Supernal Abode; the nature of the Christos.

Presence of Yahweh: A term for the Holy Shekinah; the manifest Life-power. *See also* Shekinah.

Pure Kabal: Pure or primordial tradition; pure divine revelation; an inmost secret teaching or transmission of gnosis; a term often used to designate the Melchizedek Teachings in the Sophian Tradition.

Queen of Heaven: A name of the Divine Mother or God the Mother.

Queen of the Shabbat: A name of the Holy Shekinah. See Shekinah.

Raphael: Literally, "the healing power of God"; one of the seven arch-angels of the Christos; associated with Tiferet (Beauty), the Christ Center, on the Kabbalistic Tree of Life; presides over the order of Malachim (Messengers), the sphere of the sun and element of air.

Ratziel: Literally, "the wisdom of God"; the archangel of Wisdom or Sophia; corresponds to Hokmah (Wisdom) on the Kabbalistic Tree of Life; holds dominion of the order of Ofanim (Wheels) and the sphere of the zodiac, and is said to know the inmost secrets of the Grail and the mystery of the twelve Saviors.

Rite of Ransom: The secret knowledge of the mystery of the Cruci-fixion; inner rites of initiation celebrated in Gnostic Christianity; the practice of Divine theurgy for the sake of the enlightenment and liberation of souls.

Rite of the Standing Stones and the Great Circle: A specific rite of Gnostic worship in the Sophian Tradition that celebrates the hieros gamos or sacred marriage.

Sacred Lance: The spear used to pierce the side of the Christ-bearer on the cross according to legend; a phallic symbol that is the bal-ance to the Holy Grail; a symbol of Christ the Logos.

Sandalfon: Literally, "shoe of God" or "shoe angel"; the angel of the Holy Shekinah; the archangel associated with Malkut (Kingdom) on the Kabbalistic Tree of Life and with the Spirit of the Prophets; archangel of the Divine Kingdom (generally said to be feminine); the female polarity of Metatron or twin of Metatron.

Satan: Literally, "opponent" or "adversary"; the shadow of the demi-urge; the most potent arch demon. Satan is quite distinct from the demiurge and archons in most forms of Gnostic Christianity— hence darkness versus admixture.

School of St. Lazarus (or Order of St. Lazarus): A specific body of teachings and practices within the Sophian Tradition that are con-sidered extremely esoteric and are rarely taught.

Second Adam: A term indicating the union of Christ the Logos and Christ the Sophia; the image in the bridal chamber; the power of

Lord Yeshua and Lady Mary in the sacred marriage; the realization of the Soul of Light as an androgynous and bornless being.

Second Coming: The advent of the Bride's reception and Age of the Holy Spirit; the dawn of Christ consciousness in the larger collective of humanity; the fruition of human evolution as we presently understand it.

Secret Order: The inmost circle of a Gnostic community; the order of the Sacred Tau; a term indicating the Order of Melchizedek. See Order of Melchizedek.

Serpent: A term that may indicate Satan, but also the Christos in Gnostic Christianity; also a name for Sophia in some Gnostic teachings. (The Serpent is a complex esoteric teaching in Gnosticism and not easily expressed, for it does not always represent evil as in orthodox or fundamental forms of Christianity.)

Shabbat: The day of the Beloved; a day set aside for spiritual fellowship and spiritual practice; a term for the bridal chamber.

Shekinah: The Divine presence and power of God; the feminine aspect of God; God the Mother; the Divine Consort of God; the immanent aspect of Divine Being; sometimes synonymous with the Holy Spirit.

Son of Adam: *See also* Great Seth.

Sophia Nigrans: Literally, "Black Wisdom"; the dark and wrathful aspects of Sophia; the wisdom of the darkness in the womb and mystical death; a complex array of various aspects of Divine Wisdom all having an enigmatic quality and tending to be unpredictable; aspects of Wisdom that lead to transcendence. (This is an extremely complex and esoteric subject in Sophian teachings.)

Sophia Stellarum: Literally, "Wisdom of the Stars"; the bright and peaceful or blissful aspects of Sophia; a complex array of various aspects of Divine Wisdom that tend to be more easily received and understood than those of Sophia Nigrans. According to the tradition, one cannot truly separate Sophia Stellarum from Sophia Nigrans—they are one Wisdom of God.

Sophian: An initiate of the Sophian Tradition of Gnostic Christianity; a person who believes in the coequality of Lord Yeshua and Lady Mary; a person having faith in St. Mary Magdalene or gnosis of St. Mary Magdalene; a Gnostic practitioner who is strongly founded in the Sacred Feminine.

Sorcery: Black magic; any form of psychism or magic used for selfish or destructive purposes; any use of magic that does not facilitate the great work.

Soul Mate: A soul that emanates into both a male and a female incarnation to enact a union in the world and thus extend something of the Supernal Light; souls destined to be together in union.

Soul of the World: A name of Daughter Sophia or Bride Sophia; the aspect of Sophia immanent in the world; Sophia within the collective consciousness of the world.

Spell of Death: The illusionary appearance of death as the end of life or of the soul; a term for the law according to Gnosticism.

Spirit of Holiness: See Holy Spirit.

Spirit of Truth: An alternative name for the Holy Spirit.

Spirit of Yahweh: Light-Spirit; the Holy Spirit; the Spirit of the Life-power.

Spiritual Sun: A common name for the Christos in Gnostic Christianity, which does not designate gender—hence the Sun of God rather than the "Son of God." This usage points to Christ as the Light of God or a state of Divine illumination.

St. Michael: The legendary son of Yeshua and Mary; the Light-transmission that passed into the world through the agency of Yeshua and Mary; a state of Divine illumination.

Supernal Abode: The World of Supernal Light; the bridal chamber.

Supernal Crown: Keter (Crown) on the Kabbalistic Tree of Life.

Tau: A term used for a spiritual master or realized individual in Gnostic Tradition; an elder apostle of a Gnostic lineage; an initiate whose primary task is that of an initiator and spiritual guide to others; an initiate who embodies a distinct manifestation of the Divine presence and power. In the Sophian Tradition, the Tau used is the last letter of the Hebrew alphabet, akin to Omega in Greek and connoting the same meaning. It is designated by the sign of a cross. (The actual meaning of Tau can be quite different from one Gnostic Tradition to another. Thus what is said here applies to the Sophian definition only.)

Tikkune: Literally, "correction," "repair," "mending," or "healing"; the process of development and evolution of the soul; the process of completing and perfecting creation; restoration to Sacred Unity.

True Gnosis: The state of supernal or Messianic consciousness; the state of enlightenment and liberation; complete gnosis of the Risen Savior.

Tzaddik: A term used to denote a spiritual teacher and guide among Sophians; an elder or tau of the Sophian Tradition; an initiate who has attained some degree of self-realization.

Tzadkiel: Literally, "righteousness of God"; one of the seven archangels of the Christos; corresponds to Hesed (Mercy) on the Kabbalistic Tree of Life and has dominion over the order of the Hashmalim (Speaking Silences); associated with the sphere of Jupiter.

Tzaphkiel: One of the seven archangels of the Christos; archangel of Binah (Understanding) on the Kabbalistic Tree of Life; associated with the throne of God, the planetary sphere of Saturn and the spiritual power of remembrance.

Uriel: Literally, "light of God"; one of the seven archangels of the Christos; associated with the mercy of God and the element of earth.

Virgin: The transcendent nature of Sophia.

Wedding Feast: A term for the Holy Eucharist in Gnosticism that alludes to the mystery of hieros gamos or sacred marriage behind it.

Wedding Feast of Melchizedek: The inmost secret mystery of the Gnostic Eucharist.

Whore: A term used to indicate that Sophia is immanent in all things; hence that she withholds herself from no one, not even from dark and hostile beings-forces.

Yahweh: Literally, "That Which Was, Is and Forever Shall Be"; the Light-continuum; the proper name of God in the Old Testament; the Great Name of God.

Yeshua: Aramaic for "Jesus"; literally, "Yahweh delivers." In Hebrew, it is the name Yahweh with the addition of one letter, the letter Shin, and implies one who has realized and embodied the Light-continuum.

Zion: In Gnosticism, Zion is not a physical or material place, but rather represents a spiritual state of consciousness—a state of Divine illumination.

SUGGESTED READING LIST

Barnstone, Willis, and Marvin Meyer. *The Gnostic Bible*. Boston: Shambhala Publications, 2003.

Haskins, Susan. *Mary Magdalene*. New York: HarperCollins, 1993.

Leloup, Jean-Yves. *The Gospel of Mary Magdalene*. Rochester, VT: Inner Traditions International, 2002.

———. *The Gospel of Philip*. Rochester, VT: Inner Traditions International, 2003.

Matthews, Caitlin. *Sophia:Goddess of Wisdom*. London: HarperCollins, 1991.

Meyer, Martin. *The Gospels of Mary*. San Francisco: HarperCollins, 2004.

Pagels, Elaine. *The Gnostic Gospels*. New York: Random House, 1979.

Schipflinger, Thomas. *Sophia-Maria*. York Beach, ME: Samuel Weiser, 1998.

Starbird, Margaret, *The Woman with the Alabaster Jar*. Rochester, VT: Bear & Company, 1993.

☾ LLEWELLYN ORDERING INFORMATION

Order Online:
Visit our website at www.llewellyn.com, select your books, and order them on our secure server.

Order by Phone:
- Call toll-free within the U.S. at 1-877-NEW-WRLD (1-877-639-9753). Call toll-free within Canada at 1-866-NEW-WRLD (1-866-639-9753)
- We accept VISA, MasterCard, and American Express

Order by Mail:
Send the full price of your order (MN residents add 7% sales tax) in U.S. funds, plus postage & handling to:

Llewellyn Worldwide
2143 Wooddale Drive, Dept. 0-7387-0783-X
Woodbury, Minnesota 55125-2989, U.S.A.

Postage & Handling:

Standard (U.S., Mexico, & Canada). If your order is:
$49.99 and under, add $3.00
$50.00 and over, FREE STANDARD SHIPPING

AK, HI, PR: $15.00 for one book plus $1.00 for each additional book.

International Orders (airmail only):
$16.00 for one book plus $3.00 for each additional book

Orders are processed within 2 business days.
Please allow for normal shipping time. Postage and handling rates subject to change.

TO WRITE TO THE AUTHOR

If you wish to contact the author or would like more information about this book, please write to the author in care of Llewellyn Worldwide and we will forward your request. Both the author and publisher appreciate hearing from you and learning of your enjoyment of this book and how it has helped you. Llewellyn Worldwide cannot guarantee that every letter written to the author can be answered, but all will be forwarded. Please write to:

Tau Malachi
c/o Llewellyn Worldwide
2143 Wooddale Drive, Dept. 0-7387-0783-X
Woodbury, MN 55125-2989, U.S.A.

Please enclose a self-addressed stamped envelope for reply,
or $1.00 to cover costs. If outside U.S.A., enclose
international postal reply coupon.

Many of Llewellyn's authors have websites with additional information and resources. For more information, please visit our website at http://www.llewellyn.com.